Teachers as Mentors:
A Practical Guide

Other books of particular interest are

The Return of the Mentor *edited by Brian J Caldwell and Earl M A Carter*

Mentoring in Mathematics Teaching *edited by Barbara Jaworski and Anne Watson*

Mentorship in the Primary School *edited by Robin Yeomans and John Sampson*

Teachers as Mentors:
A Practical Guide

Edited by

Barbara and Terry Field

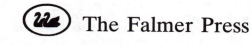 The Falmer Press

(A member of the Taylor & Francis Group)
London • Washington, D.C.

UK   The Falmer Press, 4 John Street, London WC1N 2ET
USA   The Falmer Press, Taylor & Francis Inc., 1900 Frost Road, Suite 101, Bristol, PA 19007

First published in 1994
Reprinted 1996

A catalogue record for this book is available from the British Library

Library of Congress Cataloging-in-Publication Data are available on request

ISBN 0 7507 0316 4 (cased)
ISBN 0 7507 0317 2 (paper)

Jacket design by Caroline Archer

Typeset in 11/13 pt Garamond
by Graphicraft Typesetters Ltd, Hong Kong

Printed and bound in Great Britain by Biddles Ltd, Guildford and King's Lynn on paper which has a specified pH value on final paper manufacture of not less than 7.5 and is therefore 'acid-free'.

Contents

Contents

List of Figures

Abbreviations

AST	Advanced Skills Teacher
CATE	Council for the Accreditation of Teacher Education
DES	Department of Education and Science
DfE	Department for Education
Dip.Ed	Graduate Diploma in Education
ESL	English as a Second Language
GDE	Graduate Diploma in Education
HEI	Higher Education Institution
HMI	Her Majesty's Inspector
HMSO	Her Majesty's Stationery Office
INSET	In-service Education and Training
IT	Information Technology
ITE	Initial Teacher Education
LEA	Local Education Authority
MACTEQT	Ministerial Advisory Council on Teacher Education and the Quality of Teaching
NCAT	National Curriculum Attainment Targets
NPQTL	National Project on the Quality of Teaching and Learning
NQT	Newly Qualified Teacher
OUDES	Oxford University Department of Education Studies
QTS	Qualified Teacher Status
PGCE	Post Graduate Certificate in Education
RoAD	Record of Achievement and Development
RoPA	Record of Professional Achievement
RoSE	Record of Student Experience
UEA	University of East Anglia
UNE	University of New England-Armidale

Introduction

Terry Field

Background

Pre-service teacher education is undergoing change. In the last few years, the process of the supervision of pre-service student teachers when they go into schools for a *practicum* has been transformed markedly in the United Kingdom and is under scrutiny in Australia and in the United States. In the United Kingdom the task of the supervising teachers in schools has changed. They are now asked to be real partners with departments of education in universities in the task of pre-service teacher education. By insisting on more of a school-base to teacher education, governments are asking that learning to be a teacher be more firmly contextualised in the school than it has been in the past. This book explores what it is that supervising teachers are now being asked to do, and contrasts this with what they were asked to do ten years ago.

In England and Wales in 1992 schools and Higher Education Institutions (HEIs) moved to placing students in schools for 120 days out of 180 days of the Post Graduate Certificate in Education (PGCE) course — that is, two-thirds of the PGCE course is delivered in schools by school teachers, and one-third of the course is delivered in universities by teacher education staff. In June 1993 the Secretary of State published the document that outlined how the programs of primary teacher education would also become school-based over the next two years (DfE 1993). The ramifications are enormous. The staffing of some parts of universities will be affected dramatically. The distribution of each student's grant money will be different. Even more important, the task of many teachers in schools will change. This is the focus of this book. Because student teachers are to spend most of their PGCE year with their school supervisors rather than their university tutors, teachers are having to take over much of the course content that used to be dealt with in the university. In England and Wales, teachers are finding that

1

they have to become teacher educators rather than supervisors in the former sense. The word being used to describe them and their new task is 'mentor'. Teachers in schools are now entrusted with the lion's share of educating student teachers into the teaching profession. Teachers need to know what skills and competencies should be developed by the student teachers in their care in order for them to be equipped to begin teaching in a full-time capacity, and what skills and competencies they themselves need in order to be able to mentor the student teachers appropriately and adequately. Teachers also need to study the lived experience of student teachers as they practise in schools so that they understand the feelings and fears and stresses that the students are experiencing as embryo teachers.

In Australia, documents from the Commonwealth Department of Employment, Education and Training (DEET), such as 'Teaching Counts' (1993), imply similar changes to teacher education in the future. Education Ministry documents in each State also presage more of a school base to teacher education. New South Wales Ministry of Education officers have visited CATE and the DfE in London to find out how the school-based teacher education scheme is working. There have been political moves to change the National Award for payment of teachers for supervision — a step that would be necessary if Australian teacher education were to become more school-based. Australian teachers are presently paid $21.20 per day to supervise a student under the National Practice Teaching Award. It would be prohibitive to pay this amount for 120 days of *practicum* for each student. Most pre-service teacher education programs allocate only about 40 days of *practicum* for Graduate Diploma in Education (GDE) students, not because it is believed that that is sufficient *practicum*, but because that is all that can be afforded.

Audiences

There are three specific audiences for this book — the teachers in schools who want to know more about the task of mentoring that is being asked of them; the student teachers who want to know how their teacher education courses will change and how mentoring is to be done; and the university teacher education staff who, because the teaching award is still a university award, have the responsibility of quality control and therefore of training the mentor teachers in their important role.

Structure of the Book

The first four chapters of this book deal with the issues outlined above from the perspective of both Australia and of the United Kingdom. The next four chapters are representative of the exemplary practice that is being carried out in the partnerships between schools and universities in the United Kingdom.

The first chapter looks at the problem of defining the skills and competencies for the professions and in particular those required by the beginning teacher. *Circular 9/92* confidently lists such a set of skills and competencies, and appears to expect pre-service teacher education to be competency-based. The New South Wales Ministerial Advisory Council on Teacher Education and the Quality of Teaching has also produced such a list. These lists are examined and their usefulness is explored.

The second chapter relates the lived experience of some developing student teachers using *verbatim* reports from their journals. Unless we listen to the voices of the student teachers who undergo the experiences designed for them by teacher educators and school teachers, programs of teacher education could be wide of the mark of catering for their real needs.

The third chapter deals with the past role of teachers in the supervision of students. This role concentrated on socialising the students into the profession and was one of pastoral care more than anything else. This is an important role and will continue, but in the change to a more school-based teacher education program, it is not sufficient and must now be augmented.

The fourth chapter deals with mentoring — the changed role of teachers now that more of the course is in schools rather than in the university as before. The importance of the role of the experienced practitioner in the professional development of newcomers is acknowledged in many professions, crafts and trades. As David Frost writes, 'the responsibility of the mentor teacher is that of "gate-keeper" for the profession' (1993:130). There are, and have always been, tensions, anomalies and disparities in the supervising/mentoring process. The quality of mentoring depends, as the quality of supervision has always depended, on human differences. This chapter explores ways of lessening the impact of these differences by forming working partnerships between universities and schools in producing programs of mentoring.

Chapters 5–8 deal with specific examples of mentoring as practised in schemes developed by four HEIs — Manchester, Warwick, East Anglia and York — and their partner schools . They outline exemplary programs of mentoring and partnership. They are only four of the many programs that are being worked out in universities and schools all over England. They show some ways in which imaginative and flexible thinking can meet the challenges presented in government documents, so that students in schools and student teachers are not disadvantaged by changes.

In Chapter 5 — *Towards Empowerment: An Approach to School-Based Mentoring* — David Read's emphasis is clearly stated in the title. In the chapter he details the way in which The University of Manchester and its partner schools see the new school-based program as empowering mentors and helping them to model the principles of continuous learning and reflection that they are trying to help their student teachers acquire. Read addresses the pros and cons of mentor empowerment and discusses the competences — documented in The University of Manchester *Record of Achievement and Development* (RoAD) — which are the focus of their Initial Teacher Education program.

Chris Kellett — in Chapter 6: *Towards More School-Based Initial Teacher Education* — provides a detailed description of how a school has responded to the challenges of having some of its teachers take on the additional role of teacher educators. Her position of ITE Co-ordinator in Fulford School has involved her in all stages of program development and has enabled her to write an insightful and colourful account of how problems and concerns were overcome. Of special note in this chapter is the Whole School Issues program which is an integral part of the approach to Initial Teacher Education (ITE) which has been developed by Fulford School in partnership with the University of York. Day-to-day organisation of the program is discussed so that readers can see how the program has been made to work as effectively as it has and why it is seen as exemplary.

A second university perspective is provided in Chapter 7 where Chris Husbands analyses a number of models of school-based teacher education and shows how the University of East Anglia action-research model has built on them. The emphasis here is very much on how theory and practice in teacher education have been integrated in their school-based program. This work has drawn on the writings of Stenhouse (for example, 1975) and Elliott (for example, 1990) and has involved a very close partnership with schools in the region. The essential features of student teachers' practice experience are discussed, emphasising the intimate linking of observation, practice and research, and the working together of students and teachers in interrogating practice. Husbands sees this dialogue, while problematic, as being highly productive.

The fourth 'workface' report, in Chapter 8, relates the experience of the first year of the mentoring scheme embarked on by Warwick University and its school partners. Here, Martin Robinson, the Deputy Head at Ashlawn School, is reflective in reporting in considerable detail the opinions of the University tutors and mentors and the school tutors and mentors. At the heart of this scheme, the student teachers' progress is charted — through a process of review and target-setting — in a *Record of Professional Achievement* (RoPA). A special feature of this chapter is the insight it gives into the evolution of the school-University partnership over the first year. It is a very objective report — an honest and frank appraisal — which highlights the theory-practice links also clearly featured in the three preceding chapters.

Each of these chapters draws on the experiences of a particular partnership setting. Not unnaturally, there are differences in the terminology used in them. For instance, the term *practicum* is not common among them; the term 'competences' is used more often in England than 'competencies' which is used in Australia; the labels 'professional' and 'subject' for both university tutors and school mentors are used differently and the styling of the documentation used for recording student progress is idiosyncratic. But it was seen as unnecessary and undesirable to attempt to impose an editorial uniformity on them. They are lively but differing accounts which provide many valuable insights.

Chapter 9 draws some conclusions that may be helpful for teachers who are taking on the role of mentoring in the very challenging task of pre-service teacher education. It also talks about mentoring as professional development for teachers, and as a way forward on a career path.

Why is a Change in Pre-Service Teacher Education Necessary?

Before we begin the examination of the major issues outlined above, it is best to try to give some answer to the question that is on everyone's mind: why do we need to change the way we train teachers? Has the present system not served us well for many years? Why should student teachers spend much more time in schools? Is it necessary?

At the University of New England (UNE) in northern New South Wales, in a *post-practicum* survey, students in the Bachelor of Teaching course were asked how they would react if their time in schools were to be increased to about 60 per cent of their course. At present, they do only three weeks of *practicum* in each of their first two years of study, and ten weeks in their third and final year. They spend only 25 per cent of their total course in schools. The following are typical of the overwhelming majority of replies:

Most definitely (in favour). Theory is important, but you can know all the theory and be a dreadful teacher. Practice is essential to become a competent and confident teacher.

Practice should be increased. With such a practical, demanding future career, we need to see children in action, how the classroom works, problems — not just know what the textbook says.

I believe the only way to become a good teacher is through experience.

Fifty per cent would be a lot better as I find I learn a lot more in the classroom with the children than I do talking about it at university.

We need to be in the classroom. What better way to learn about teaching children than to be in the classroom experiencing it first hand — not hearing about it second hand.

I have learnt a lot more in practice teaching than I have in lectures.

I believe we should spend more time school based. This is where we get our experience. The three weeks we had this year were not nearly long enough. I had an excellent practicum but I would have loved to spend the rest of the term — or the year — at the school.

As most teachers and lecturers tell us, children learn by doing — so do student teachers.

The above responses give one answer to the question: Why is a change necessary — why has more of a school-base been introduced to Initial Teacher Education? Students are adamant that they need to be in schools as much as possible. When student teachers are asked what part of their pre-service teacher education course was of most help in their movement along the continuum from being 'not-a-teacher' to being 'a teacher', they invariably say that it was in their school experiences that they learnt the most about teaching. They feel strongly that it is better for them to be in schools learning how to teach than in university learning about teaching.

Another answer to the question is given in *Circular 9/92* which says that the change to more school-based teacher education is necessary to improve the quality of teaching in schools. Universities, rightly or wrongly, are seen as remote from the practical task that they are teaching about. Students tend to indicate that the *practicum* is a matter of survival when they have only three or four weeks each year in a school. There is more of a professional growth factor when they have a more substantial time in a school with an experienced, committed mentor teacher.

Many metaphors of the *practicum* come through in the literature. From computing we get the metaphor that the *practicum* is a time when a young student teacher is allowed to 'recover gracefully from mistakes'. From gardening we find that the *practicum* is a time when young student teachers 'bloom' and 'blossom'. From drama we use the term 'rehearsing' the skills and competencies of teaching. Whatever metaphor is used, the mentor (a metaphor in itself) is the chief instrument in the processes of the *practicum*, and it is mentoring that is the major concern of this book.

Chapter 1

The Skills and Competencies of Beginning Teachers

Barbara Field

There are two tasks to do before we try to identify the skills and competencies needed by a teacher to be a successful mentor under a school-based system of teacher education. There are two underpinning areas of understanding that will inform our judgment and conclusions. The first of these is the analysis of the various attempts to identify the skills and competencies necessary in a beginning teacher, and the second is the gaining of an understanding of the lived experience of student teachers as they practise in a school. This chapter deals with the first of these. Chapter 2 explores the experience of student teachers revealed through their own professional diaries and journals.

Introduction

The definition of a beginning teacher to be used in this chapter is a teacher who has completed a course of teacher education at a Higher Education Institution and is embarking, newly-employed, on a teaching career. The definition of 'competencies' is 'the types of skill, knowledge and attitudes that will form the basis of effective professional practice'. Walker developed the following definition of 'competence':

> The attributes (knowledge, skills, attitudes) which enable an individual or group to perform a role or set of tasks to an appropriate level or grade of quality or achievement (ie an appropriate standard) and thus make the individual or group *competent* in that role. (1992:1–2)

The point to keep in mind in the discussion of skills and competencies for a profession, as opposed to a trade or craft, is that often the skills and competencies for a profession cannot be assessed with any degree of objectivity or accuracy. It is easy to judge if an apprentice student can measure the thickness of a piece of copper wire to a certain degree of accuracy, and a mark can be awarded for the performance of the task; but it is not equally easy to judge if a student teacher has an understanding of the National Curriculum, and very difficult to give a mark or a grade to this. One skill can be observed. The other has to be inferred. Similarly, it is easier to judge whether a student teacher is able to write coherent lesson plans than it is to judge whether a student teacher has an understanding of the school as an institution.

In Australia, the National Training Board has been given the task of developing national standards of competency for trades. But the task of developing competency lists for the professions has been given to the National Office of Overseas Skills Recognition (NOOSR). NOOSR is the group that assesses the qualifications of professional people who have been trained overseas and who want to practise in Australia. They have the experience of working with the more ephemeral skills and competencies that pertain to the professions. Nursing was the first profession for which competencies were identified, and the Nursing Competencies Assessment Project (NCAP) concluded that, 'there are relevant and practicable methods for the compilation of valid lists of competencies for the profession' (NOOSR 1990:17). However, they also acknowledge that 'lists of competencies can never be set in stone. Knowledge and expertise change and grow. The professional is committed to lifelong learning — which is an attribute clearly identified in the lists of competencies' (NOOSR 1990:17).

One of the reasons for the identification and assessment in the professions is the emphasis on quality assurance that has swept the professions in the last decade. Included in this movement has been world-wide interest in monitoring the quality of teaching, and one of the ways that governments have adopted for attempting to improve the quality of teaching performance is to list the skills and competencies needed to carry out the task effectively.

At the time of writing (1993), there are many groups in Britain and in Australia working on the identification of the skills and competencies of beginning teachers. Some of these are recorded in this chapter. They all acknowledge that the competence of a beginning teacher is different from that of a teacher at the end of the induction year or that of an experienced teacher. There are certain skills necessary for survival in the classroom at the beginning of a career in teaching. These skills mature and develop as the teacher grows in the profession. It is the skills for beginning teachers that mentor teachers must have in mind as they guide the practising students towards professional competence. A student teacher cannot be expected to act with the degree of competence of a teacher of ten years' experience. Learning to teach is a process and there are stages that the student teacher and the beginning teacher must be allowed to move through.

The identification of competencies is a beneficial exercise that can enhance the educational processes that should lead to the attainment of these competencies. A knowledge of the skills and competencies for beginning teachers could be used as an important focus for mentor teachers. A framework of competencies can give guidance for the teacher education program in the school. For the mentor teacher, reflection on lists of skills and competencies for beginning teachers could be a fruitful way into identifying how the task of the mentor teacher now differs from the task of the supervising teacher in the past.

The accurate and fair assessment of competencies for a profession such as teaching is more problematic than the identification of such competencies. Usually, a list of competencies implies an accompanying list of levels of competence. For teachers writing reports on student teachers for a practice teaching session, this kind of quantitative assessment becomes difficult to determine. Parity across schools and different supervisors is difficult to achieve. However, given these problems, lists of competencies can prove useful as a focus for a School Experience Curriculum, and certainly it is necessary for mentor teachers to know the expectations for students at various levels of their program.

When the education of student teachers is shared between schools and Higher Education Institutions with most of the time being spent in schools, the question of the division of responsibilities will always arise — which institution is responsible for the student teacher's attaining each of the skills and competencies? Which are combined responsibilities? Who teaches the students to write lesson notes, for example? Who is responsible for classroom management strategies? Can these be taught out of context? Who teaches the subject method? These are some of the questions that have to be resolved in the partnerships that are developing between schools and university Departments of Education. There are some answers to these questions in Chapters 5–8.

Lists of Competencies for Beginning Teachers

The various lists of competencies for beginning teachers that have been produced by government bodies in the last two years are, of necessity, of generic competencies. The notion of generic competencies is problematic. It implies that the skills and competencies 'apply in all settings and contexts, at all levels and to all modes of teaching' (NPQTL 1993:3). The competencies are meant to apply to all beginning teachers, from early childhood teachers to senior secondary teachers. The notion assumes that there are core skills in what is required in competent teaching irrespective of subject content, student's characteristics and specific school context. We are making that difficult assumption in this chapter with the acknowledgment that teaching is a complex process and that sensible judgments cannot be made about a teacher's attainment of any competence without taking into account the social context, the individual characteristics of the teacher and the nature of the students to be taught. There are, of course, specific competencies that apply to the specific subject areas in the curriculum. These are being researched by subject specialists. We are dealing here only with generic competencies.

One advantage of a list of skills and competencies for beginning teachers is that such a list makes public the nature and tasks of teaching. It makes explicit the areas of competency expected of a beginning teacher. It opens to scrutiny the practice of teachers as measured against the list. In an era when accountability and quality control are of such importance, this can be an advantage to the employer, the pupil and the teacher. The improvement of teaching that can be effected within the framework of the competencies will also improve the learning that takes place, and this, after all, is what our schools are about — effective learning.

Competencies considered important enough to be included are usually demonstrable or at least observable. If they cannot be operationalised or observed, it becomes very difficult to assess them, or report on them, objectively. The following lists of skills and competencies should be scrutinised for this demonstrability. For example, the first sub-heading in the list from the Ministerial Advisory Council *The Ethics of Teaching* has been criticised for not being demonstrable (see p. 16). How does one demonstrate belief, especially if the demonstration is to be measured?

Most Higher Education Institutions with a program of Initial Teacher Education would have, in their guides for supervising teachers, a list of generic target skills and competencies expected of the student teacher. The University of Cambridge Department of Education has a comprehensive check list headed *Teaching Competences* (1992–1993). It has detailed elements under nine headings. Only the headings are given here, but the detailed elements under each are most searching:

1 Relationships with pupils (In both the pastoral and the teaching context)

2   Subject knowledge (Students' competence in their own field of knowledge)
3   Planning (Preparing individual lessons and curriculum units)
4   Class management (Organising the learning environment)
5   Communication
6   Assessment (Assessing, recording and interpreting pupil performance)
7   Reflecting on practice (Evaluating one's own teaching and modifying professional practice)
8   Professionalism (Setting and maintaining appropriate standards of professional behaviour)
9   Personal qualities

Government Departments of Education are joining in the devising of lists of competencies. One government document that has outlined skills and competencies for beginning teachers is the former Department of Education and Science's (DES) *Reform of Teacher Education*. This was published on 28 January 1992, following the North of England Conference speech by Kenneth Clark, then Secretary of State for Education, in which he outlined proposed changes to initial teacher education. In *Annex II* to the DES document, the competences expected of newly qualified teachers (that is, of those students graduating from a pre-service or initial teacher education program) were listed.

Circular 9/92 from the Department for Education (DfE) (June 1992) was a follow-up publication to the discussion document above, and under the heading 'Competences expected of newly qualified teachers' it lists almost exactly the criteria of the DES document. The few changes[1] were mainly a result of government documents that had appeared after the publication of *Reform of Teacher Education* and of responses to the call for consultation. The *Circular 9/92 list* is produced in full below:

2.2   Subject Knowledge

Newly qualified teachers should be able to demonstrate:
2.2.1   an understanding of the knowledge, concepts and skills of their specialist subjects and of the place of these subjects in the school curriculum;
2.2.2   knowledge and understanding of the National Curriculum and attainment targets (NCATs) and the programs of study (PoS) in the subjects they are preparing to teach, together with an understanding of the framework of the statutory requirements;

2.2.3 a breadth and depth of subject knowledge extending beyond programs of study and examination of syllabuses in school.

2.3 Subject Application

Newly qualified teachers should be able to:

2.3.1 produce coherent lesson plans which take account of NCATs and of the school's curriculum policies;

2.3.2 ensure continuity and progression within and between classes and in subjects;

2.3.3 set appropriately demanding expectations for pupils;

2.3.4 employ a range of teaching strategies appropriate to the age, ability and level of pupils;

2.3.5 present subject content in clear language and in a stimulating manner;

2.3.6 contribute to the development of pupils' language and communication skills;

2.3.7 demonstrate ability to select and use appropriate resources, including Information Technology.

2.4 Class Management

Newly qualified teachers should be able to:

2.4.1 decide when teaching the whole class, groups, pairs, or individuals is appropriate for particular learning purposes;

2.4.2 create and maintain a purposeful and orderly environment for the pupils;

2.4.3 devise and use appropriate rewards and sanctions to maintain an effective learning environment;

2.4.4 maintain pupil's interest and motivation.

2.5 Assessment and Recording of Pupils' Progress

Newly qualified teachers should be able to:

2.5.1 identify the current level of attainment of individual pupils using NCATs, statements of attainment and end of key stage statements where applicable;

2.5.2 judge how well each pupil performs against the standard expected of a child of that age;

2.5.3 assess and record systematically the progress of individual pupils;

2.5.4 use such assessment in their teaching;

2.5.5   demonstrate that they understand the importance of reporting to pupils on their progress and of marking their work regularly against agreed criteria.

2.6   Further Professional Development

Newly qualified teachers should have acquired in initial training the necessary foundation to develop:

2.6.1   an understanding of the school as an institution and its place within the community;

2.6.2   a working knowledge of their pastoral, contractual, legal and administrative responsibilities as teachers;

2.6.3   an ability to develop effective working relationships with professional colleagues and parents, and to develop their communication skills;

2.6.4   an awareness of individual differences, including social, psychological, developmental and cultural dimensions;

2.6.5   the ability to recognise diversity of talent including that of gifted children;

2.6.6   the ability to identify special educational needs or learning difficulties;

2.6.7   a self-critical approach to diagnosing and evaluating pupils' learning, including a recognition of the effects on that learning of teachers' expectations;

2.6.8   a readiness to promote the moral and spiritual well-being of pupils.

If the main headings of the list of competencies for beginning teachers from *Circular 9/92* are compared with those of the Cambridge document, it can be seen that there is a similarity. There is, in fact, a finite and limited number of areas of criteria that beginning teachers can be expected to master. All state that student teachers should be able to relate well to pupils, know their subjects, be able to plan and assess learning units, and manage classes. All expect a degree of professionalism in the students' attitudes and practices. The lists differ mainly in the amount of detail under each. There is no suggestion that each criterion requires the same emphasis and there is no indication of how judgments should be made as to whether the criterion has been reached.

The process of constructing check lists of generic skills and competencies for beginning teachers is going on in Australia. Several studies have been carried out in the last two years. One framework was developed by the New South Wales Department of School Education in a document entitled *Teacher Entry-Level Competencies* (May 1992). Under the heading *The Key Purpose of a Teacher in the Department of School Education* the document has a general statement and then lists ten competencies:

To develop in students knowledge, skills and attitudes, to enhance their quality of life and contribution to society:

Units of Teacher Competency
1   Identify student learning needs;
2   Design program to meet learning needs;
3   Implement programs to meet learning needs;
4   Assess student learning;
5   Record and report student outcomes;
6   Evaluate programs;
7   Manage learning and information resources;
8   Participate in the life of the school;
9   Fulfil the teacher's duty of care;
10   Identify aspects of professionalism in teachers;

Again the similarity to the two previous lists can be seen. Each of these units is developed under a heading, 'Elements of Competency'. For example, under number 1, *Identify student learning needs*, there are three elements of competency:

1.1   identify the essential features of major learning theories;
1.2   identify the essential features of student development;
1.3   articulate a personal theory of how students learn.

Another proposed framework of areas of competence was constructed by a working party set up by the New South Wales Minister for Education in 1992. It has resulted in the 1993 paper by the NSW Ministerial Advisory Council on Teacher Education and Quality of Teaching, *Framework of Areas of Competence for Beginning Teachers*. It, too, is a checklist of competencies. It is reproduced here in full so that comparisons can be made with the list from *Circular 9/92*. The lists are very similar. The Australian list adds a separate section for 'The Ethics of Teaching' and has, in a separate section — 'Interaction with parents and the community' — the skills that the English document places under 2.6, 'Further professional development'. However, five of the six sections in the Australian document are similar to the five sections in the English document. Close scrutiny, however, reveals important differences. For example, the English document is obviously driven by the work being done by schools on the National Curriculum and National Assessment. The New South Wales document is not a national document. It applies only to one state — New South Wales.

Framework of Areas of Competence

1 The Ethics of Teaching

All beginning teachers should be able to demonstrate that they:

a believe that all their students have a capacity to learn and should be treated justly and equitably;

b are alert to the consequences of their own behaviour and encourage students to develop the same awareness;

c recognise and appreciate the values held by individual students, by parents, by groups of students and by the school's/centre's community; including how those values vary and how they relate to teachers' values and the work of the school;

d understand that they have a responsibility for their students' well-being;

e understand the responsibilities and obligations of belonging to the profession of teaching.

2 The Content of Teaching

All beginning teachers need to:

a have a strong and developed knowledge and understanding of content of what they have to teach and how the subject matter changes over time;

b have an understanding of learning and teaching as preparation of students for lifelong learning, and for developing and upgrading skills areas in a range of occupational categories including vocational employment opportunities;

c have an understanding of how students develop and how they learn;

d show developing skills in adapting their teaching to suit the learning needs of their students in the context in which they are teaching

    — girls;

    — gifted and talented students;

— Aboriginal and Torres Straight Island students;
— students with disabilities, learning difficulties or behaviour disorders;
— students from low socio-economic backgrounds;
— students from background languages other than English;
— students living in isolated areas;
— students from varied religious backgrounds;
— students in crisis;

e   are able to incorporate the teaching of literacy and numeracy skills regardless of the subject or age group being taught;
f   have developing knowledge about the purposes, nature and uses of a wide variety of assessment strategies;
g   have developing knowledge and understanding of the nature, sources and application of learning and information resources;
h   are aware of and show developing capacity in the use of new information technologies in educational contexts;
i   have developing competencies in recognising and valuing the experiences students bring from their lives outside the classroom, such as linguistic and cultural differences.

3   The Practice of Teaching

All beginning teachers should be able to demonstrate that they:

a   use the English language to communicate clearly and effectively, both orally and in writing, in the range of roles and contexts occurring within the classroom and the school community;
b   are aware that their own use of language is a model for bilingual students which may not be available in other domains in students' lives;
c   are developing competences in the recognition and appreciation of variants of English;
d   can establish and maintain a school and classroom learning environment which is:
       — interesting and challenging;
       — orderly and purposeful;
       — safe and supportive;
       — positive and enjoyable;
       — fostering independence, responsibility and creativity;
e   are able to improve learning outcomes for all students by

the implementation of an increasingly wide range of teaching approaches and strategies that provide alternatives to transmission teaching, and reflect contemporary, mainstream theory and practice to achieve desired learning outcomes by:

- developing competence in recognising and adapting teaching practice to different learning styles;
- varying interactive levels with the nature of the task;
- collaborative and co-operative learning;
- communicative approaches to language learning;
- differentiated curriculum materials;
- drama method (enactments, role plays, simulation, gaming);
- negotiated learning and peer assessment;
- applications of accelerated learning theory (brain compatible learning, multiple intelligences, learning styles);

f   are beginning to develop a wide range of teaching approaches and strategies that reflect contemporary, mainstream theory and practice to achieve desired learning outcomes by:

- motivating and engaging students;
- effective structuring of learning tasks;
- establishing for students expectations that are clear, challenging and achievable;
- monitoring and assessing student progress consistently and providing genuine feedback to students and parents on that progress;
- increasing learners' own source of responsibility for learning and monitoring of learning;
- evaluating the appropriateness, effectiveness and efficiency of their teaching programs.

g   can undertake classroom roles additional to that of the teacher as transmitter of information such as facilitator, director, conferencer, organiser, writer and resource person;

h   are working as part of a community team and with appropriate support and guidance developing the necessary skills to work effectively in the team with their colleagues and communicate clearly with students and parents:

- the broad intentions of any unit or segment of learning;
- an outline of the content of that unit or segment;

—what work is expected of the student;

—how the progress/development of students is to be assessed and the relationship between assessment and the teaching/learning program;

—students' progress;

—the relevance of resources;

i   reflect critically on their teaching practices and seek feedback;

j   believe in and be able to justify the value of what they teach;

k   show developing competencies in program planning and maintenance of adequate records.

4   Interaction with Parents and the School Community

Beginning teachers should be able to demonstrate that they:

a   recognise their part in the collective responsibility in development of the school or centre and its relationship with the wider emotional needs of their children;

b   consult appropriately with parents concerning the academic, social and emotional needs of their children;

c   recognise the home as the foundation of learning, and its continuing significance in student learning.

5   Professionalism and Professional Development

Beginning teachers should be able to demonstrate that they:

a   participate in a range of professional development activities as part of their continuing professional development;

b   appreciate the collegial nature of teachers' work by being able to work effectively as members of a team, understanding the role of specialist teachers in the school;

c   have a developing knowledge of the framework of law regulations and policies that affect teachers' work.

Lists of competencies such as the above can be useful because they focus upon and raise awareness of generic skills and competencies. They can be used as a yard-stick against which to assess teacher education courses. They act as a stimulus for those who are constructing and conducting courses for teacher education, both teachers in schools and teachers in Higher Education Institutions. However, they lose their usefulness if attempts are made to quantify the competency.

The list is certainly not intended to be used for assessment or registration purposes. And it is unquestionably a checklist which, by its nature, omits the complexity of human difference. The more detail it contains, the more rigid and prescriptive it becomes, and so it is important that it be kept brief and general. Smith and Alred (1993:104) object to such lists on the grounds that they do not encompass integrity, patience, philosophy of education, enjoying the company of the young and a love of (not just a knowledge of) subject.

Another Approach to Identifying Competencies

Another very different model of competency identification was used by researchers in the Australian project entitled: *The Development of National Competency Standards for Teaching, Phase 1* (NPQTL) 1993. In this project, a research group in each of three states of Australia addressed the task of identifying generic competencies for the beginning teacher. Their research methodology varied from illustrative case studies (story-telling) to critical incident workshops, and took account of the integrated, rich and complex nature of teachers' work. They all avoided the 'check-list' of competencies that researchers can be seduced into building, and which can be seen in the examples from both England and Australia quoted above. They acknowledged that, because teaching is such a complex activity, rules, as exemplified in check lists, can never account for every instance. Atomising the teaching task in this way is seen as artificial. Teaching is a task that involves constantly making choices, making decisions, solving individual problems and exercising judgment. Lists of competencies can appear not to deal with the individual context. The context is important. The nature of teaching and teachers' knowledge do not sit comfortably in the framework of a list of rules. The team of researchers who did the 'story-telling' project for NPQTL said the following:

> Teaching requires mastery of a body of knowledge to be taught but it also requires the development of a much more personal body of knowledge about [such things] as, what is worth teaching, which ways of teaching work for the teacher and what [it is that] particular students want to learn. Much of what experienced teachers know about teaching is learned on the job and is [constantly being] modified in the light of experience. The carefully polished routines and patterns of practice which

embody a teacher's knowledge of teaching are rarely made explicit. When teachers' knowledge is made explicit, [by researchers, for example] there are few points of universal agreement about what counts as effective practice.

The implication of this view of teaching and teachers' knowledge is that competence cannot adequately be defined by a list of frequently attempted tasks, preferred teaching strategies or ideal attributes of practitioners. (NPQTL 1993:4)

Their method is one of description of the 'key and essential elements of teachers' work' rather than listing teacher attributes. The mentor teacher while supervising practice teaching has the task of judging the student teacher against the 'key and essential' elements.

The NPQTL researchers have written short incidents and stories for each element that illustrate the kaleidoscope of skills and competencies that teachers, particularly beginning teachers, must exhibit in day-to-day interaction in the classroom. These cameos are grouped under five broad headings each with its 'elements' and 'performance criteria':

	ELEMENTS
Teaching Practice	Knows the content and can justify its value;
	Knows and uses a wide range of teaching strategies;
	Structures learning tasks effectively;
	Demonstrates flexibility and responsiveness.
Student Needs	Understands how students develop and how they learn;
	Recognises and responds to individual differences;
	Fosters independent learning;
	Believes that all students have the right to learn;
	Takes action to eliminate discrimination and harassment.
Relationships	Develops positive relationships with students;
	Sets and maintains clear expectations;
	Manages student behaviour firmly, fairly and consistently;

	Works collaboratively with other teachers and ancillary staff; Communicates effectively with parents (and others responsible for the care of students).
Planning and Evaluating	Plans a comprehensive learning program; Knows and uses a wide range of assessment strategies; Monitors student progress and provides feedback on progress; Reports on student progress to parents (and others responsible for the care of students); Reviews the effectiveness of teaching and learning programs.
Professional Responsibilities	Contributes to school-wide activities; Understands the framework of law and regulations affecting teacher's work; Strives to improve the quality of teaching and learning; Continues to develop professional skills.

This list is similar to the broad categories of each of the lists of competencies that we have encountered so far. But the stories attached to each of the elements make all the difference. Instead of an arid list of teacher attributes there is an anecdote that is easy for teachers and student teachers to identify with. Acknowledging, as has been said, that teaching is a human activity with as many variations as that allows in its complex nature, the researchers give examples of 'real life' teaching practice from which readers may deduce skills and competencies. The following is one example of this (NPQTL 1993:25).

1 Teaching Practice

Element   *Performance criteria*

1.4: Demonstrates flexibility and responsiveness
- Recognises learning opportunities in issues raised by students;
- Explains and modifies tasks when necessary;

That's what I eat

The aim of Ann's Year 3 science lesson was to help students distinguish between carnivores, herbivores and omnivores. Recognising her students' intense interest in dinosaurs, Ann introduced the lesson with an audio-tape called, 'We sing dinosaurs'. One of the songs includes a chant:

> Carnivore, carnivore, what do you eat?
> Arrh! Meat, meat, that's what I eat.

The tape was accompanied by a line drawing of three dinosaurs seated around a table eating their respective dinners. The children were entranced by the song and the drawing. As they coloured in the handout of the dinosaur dinner, many of the children quietly chanted the song to themselves. Throughout the day, Ann caught snatches of the song breaking through other activities.

The next day the children wanted to listen to the tape again. Ann was sorry that she had not brought it to class, and continued with the lessons she had planned. Later that morning Ann was working on language activities with a group of children with limited formal language skills. The dinosaur chant was still breaking through, and on an impulse Ann chanted:

> 'Andrew, Andrew, what do you eat?'

Andrew chanted back:

> 'Pizza, and junk food, that's what I eat.'

Ann continued around the circle, and other children joined in the chant:

> 'Fish and chips and chicken, that's what I eat'

> 'Chocolate cake and chips, that's what I eat.'

Ann abandoned her previous lesson plan and began to use the chant as the basis for a new whole language activity. The children each wrote their own chant on a large card and then drew themselves at dinner, eating the food they had written about. The class now is using the cards and chants as the basis for next month's assembly item.

This kind of case study, critical incident, or story telling, allows the supervising teacher to deduce the skills that it is illustrating and to discuss these with the student teacher. It is another method of using criteria apart from the check-list. A mentor teacher could use the story with a student teacher or a group of student teachers, as an example of an aspect of teaching that the student needs to concentrate on.

The performance criteria are placed at the top of each story to focus thinking about a specific competency. The stories demonstrate the competency. The story allows inferences to be drawn in relation to that competency and the extent to which the student teacher has developed towards it. The process of association that takes place as readers identify with the situation in the story helps to make the complexity of teaching practice accessible in terms of its component parts. The stories illustrate realistic expectations for beginning teachers. All of the examples used are real life examples that a beginning teacher could encounter. Because they are told in story language, not educational jargon, they are appropriate to an audience of beginning teachers.

There are twenty-three stories in all in this project. They illustrate sixty performance criteria — two or three for each story. These are manageable bites for discussion and critique purposes in a school's teacher education program.

The task of the mentor teacher is ultimately one of assessment of the competencies of individual student teachers. The mentor has to decide whether student teachers are sufficiently competent to be allowed to have the responsibility of a class of their own. Many competencies, although demonstrable or observable do not admit of quantitative measurement. So modes of assessment of competence will vary. If a student demonstrates 'natural' ability and competence in the areas identified in the various frameworks, there is little problem except to decide on the degree of competence if that is what is required by the local assessment system. If, however, the student teacher does not demonstrate competence in one or several of the areas of competence identified in the frameworks, the mentor teacher has the difficult task of deciding whether the practising student 'at risk' is remediable, or not capable of reaching a satisfactory level of competence.

In a practice situation, student teachers usually have a reduced load of classes and so have a little more time than a full-time teacher has for preparation and reflection. However, a month or two later, on their first appointment, beginning teachers usually have the same workload as a teacher with ten years of experience. Yet the list of skills and competencies must widen as the teacher gains experience. Therefore, as has been said, when assessing student teachers, mentor teachers must keep in mind that the skills and competencies of beginning teachers are different from those of the teacher at the end of the induction year and those of an experienced teacher.

To Sum Up

Frameworks of skills and competencies for beginning teachers imply that all people are the same and can be made to fit a common mould. But teaching is a complex activity and beginning teachers are complex human beings. Teaching is an holistic activity, not easily divided into separate components. Learning, too, is a complex activity and it is not always possible to determine why learning does or does not take place. Some would claim that teacher's work cannot be defined accurately or satisfactorily, and this makes difficult the task of judging whether a suitable standard of competence has been reached by an individual.

Given all the above, and however unsatisfactory we think the lists of competencies to be, the importance of this chapter is to focus the thinking of the mentor teacher on how we want the student teacher to be at the end of the teacher education program in the school and at the beginning of their career in the teaching profession. The examples of the inventories of criteria given in this chapter will each be more or less useful to individual needs. Whichever list a mentor teacher and a Higher Education Institution might choose to work with in partnership, such a focus for the elements of the teacher education program in the school should benefit student teachers in their professional development.

Note

1   For example, 2.6.4 was added, it would appear, as a result of responses from universities, who see their contribution in the areas of sociology, psychology and philosophy as important. 2.6.8 was added, it would appear, as a response to submissions from schools and institutions with a religious emphasis.

Chapter 2

Towards Understanding the Lived Experience of Practising Student Teachers

Barbara Field

Introduction

> Student teaching was defined as an act of endurance . . . 'trial and error', 'sink or swim', and 'baptism of fire' . . . and the mistaken assumption that sheer persistency makes a teacher. (Britzman 1991:89)

Teachers who undertake the responsibility of mentoring a student teacher during a practice teaching session should have some understanding of how student teachers feel in their role as developing teachers in a school environment. One way to know this is to ask student teachers to reflect on, and articulate, their experience during the *practicum*, and then to listen carefully to the voices of these students in their reflective journals. The discourse of endurance that is revealed in the quotation above is something of which supervising/mentoring teachers should be aware as they take upon themselves the task of judge as well as mentor.

A study carried out at the University of New England in Armidale, NSW, asked students to reflect on the processes and practices of becoming a teacher during practice teaching in a school. Each was a graduate student enrolled in the Graduate Diploma of Education which is a one-year, end-on teacher education course — the Australian equivalent of the English Post Graduate Certificate in Education (PGCE) course. Ten students were asked to keep a daily journal during their four-week block of school experience — two men and eight women. The two men did not do the exercise at all. Each of the eight women carried it out with conscientiousness, insight and thoroughness. I asked them to dialogue in the journal with their teacher, if possible (Fishman and Rower 1989). This needed some careful and sensitive negotiation between the supervising teacher and the student teacher. Some teachers are quite apprehensive about writing their thoughts about teaching. I suggested that the student write in the journal and give the journal to the teacher for a response to their entry. As predicted, some teachers did not want to dialogue with the students in their journals. Other teachers were prepared to do this, but did not write very much. In fact, the dialoguing part of the project was not very successful. This warrants its own study. Teachers need to be encouraged to be articulate about what they do very well but take for granted.

A reason for the teachers' reticence at putting their thoughts about teaching into writing could be that the concern of the classroom teacher has been typically the learning of their pupils in their classrooms, not the process of learning to teach. For student teachers, on the other hand, the concern is typically the process of learning to teach. The 'what' and 'how' of teaching seem to be their chief concerns. The student teacher's concerns, in the process of mentoring, must become the concerns of the classroom teacher.

For both the mentor teacher and the student teacher there is a learning task to be done — that of learning to talk about the teaching/learning process in a way that is helpful to the professional development of the student teacher. Both need to become 'fluent' in the language of reflection. They need to be able to talk about the specifics of teaching/learning as they critique lessons and other school experiences. The 'talk', in the task of teacher education that mentoring entails, needs to be more thorough, structured and developmental than the casual evaluations that often, in the past, have constituted 'supervision'.

Reflection on Teaching — Dialogue Journals

The keeping of a journal encouraged the students to be reflective about their practice. There has been much talk and research in recent years on reflection in teaching and about reflective teaching (see Calderhead and Gates 1993, and Elliott 1993). Reflection is a special way of thinking. It is more than 'thinking about'. It is an active and deliberate consideration of what is usually taken for granted. From the excerpts from student journals recorded below, reflection appeared often to involve the perception of problems and the devising of ways to solve those problems. Students, as evidenced in the journal data included in this chapter, are clearly concentrating on the technical and craft skills of teaching. These are uppermost in their minds as embryo teachers. Yet they also make academic and professional observations of the processes they are experiencing. The journal writing demanded a meta-cognitive skill — that of knowing about knowing. The student teachers were building on and drawing from their theoretical studies at university and what these had taught them about teaching. They were forced to articulate what they know about teaching and learning and then to apply it to the practical situation. The reflective journal is more than a description of what happened. As they reflect, student teachers can be observed testing the relationship between the rhetoric of educational theory and the reality of educational practice in classrooms. It is a 'conscious, purposeful process' (Hughes 1991:97) that delves more deeply than superficial description. It is a process that practising students are not always encouraged to take part in by their supervisors.

In the *verbatim* quotations below, the student teachers can be observed in the process which John Locke calls 'the notice which the mind takes of its own operations' (Hughes 1991:96). They are watching themselves attempting to teach and watching their own reactions to what is happening to them. They are involved with 'reflection-in-action' and 'reflection-on-action' (Schon 1983). Someone has said that practice teaching is 'knowing in action'. In writing their journals, the students had to stand back and observe, objectively, their practice, analyse and critique it, and come up with resolutions, explanations and clarifications of the processes.

Students and teachers need to be taught how to be reflective — how to stand back and observe objectively what they are experiencing, or have experienced, and then be able to talk about it. Mentor teachers, particularly, should be able to interrogate their own teaching practice and examine the contexts in which teaching is embedded. But reflection needs to be guided. Student teachers need to have focus points on which they can concentrate. These can be actual aspects of their own classroom behaviour such as managing different kinds of pedagogy (small groups or whole class), introducing a lesson, explaining a point, questioning or concluding a session. They could, on the other hand, be areas of experience such as the management strategies for gaining and holding attention, pacing lessons appropriately, having resource material to hand, being able to deal with both major and minor interruptions and misbehaviour and the social and psychological elements that are impinging on the context of a particular classroom. Some students intuitively know these focuses, others need to be coached into them.

The study showed that thoughtful, committed student teachers, when asked to keep dialogue journals, reveal an incisive insight into their practice. In the first journal extracts below, the students are showing that they can observe themselves objectively. They can see that they are not making the contacts with the students, not communicating in the way they want to, and they are suggesting tentative solutions to the problem. Students are, in fact, devastatingly honest about their own practice, if they have a trusted audience to confide in. However, they do tend to highlight the faults in their teaching. Students, when asked at the end of a lesson, 'How do you think that went?' will invariably react with negative responses. This points to the need, in conferencing, for the mentor teacher to ask first, 'What do you think went well in that lesson?' The students in the study were open and honest about their reactions, day-by-day, to classroom teaching and their perceptions of their own professional movement from being 'not-a-teacher' to 'being-a-teacher'.

The Responding Students

The eight women students who participated in the project are very different in their backgrounds and personality:

Ailsa is a very serious student. She gives the impression, at the age of twenty-one, of being a teacher of ten years experience. She is sensible and reliable and very thoughtful about her practice.

Mandy is a bright, cheery lass carrying the burden of a very sick mother. She almost had to abandon her *practicum*, but special arrangements were made for her to do her *practicum* near her mother. She was a graduate student doing primary methods.

Christine is a single parent, with two under-fives. She had always espoused a socialist ethic which she found sorely tested by behaviour problems in schools. She is also a committed feminist. She taught English and history.

Lisa is like a fragile English rose. She speaks with a very clipped English accent. She had found in her previous *practicum* that her discipline was affected by these attributes. She taught English and so had to cope with large classes. She anticipates that she would be best to teach in a private girls' school.

Jane is a student that I had taught at school, and I think she did the exercise only to please me. I felt that her heart was not in it as much as the others. She taught Japanese and ESL, so she had smaller classes than, for example, the students who taught English.

Trish is an outgoing student — full of naive enthusiasm and positive attitudes. She is prepared to try anything that would further
her professional development. Her infectious joy about everything
in life is a great asset for teaching. She taught English and ESL.

Rachel is another bright and positive student, not as naive as Trish,
a little steadier and as committed. She taught English and Drama.

Alice is the weakest of the eight students. She had had some problems in her previous *practicum* with discipline. I sometimes felt
that she had some doubts about taking up teaching as a career.
She taught English.

The students covered a wide range of discourses in their journal
entries. They ranged across areas from their own professional development, through praxis-shock, stress, the shortcomings of their supervising teacher and their relationships with pupils, to the need to make
theory/practice links.

Practical Skills

Graduate Diploma in Education students always feel that the university
does not prepare them adequately for the practical skills that they
need in the classroom. The first extracts below show students grappling
with the problem of using effectively the craft skills of questioning and
explaining:

> I think I need to structure the lessons more thoroughly so that each
> question is leading somewhere or developing an overall concept.
> (Christine)

> It was extremely rewarding to have attentive and enthusiastic stu-
> dents. On reflection I feel that the key to this success was keeping
> the group busy on a variety of different activities. I need to im-
> prove my questioning techniques. I need to draw out answers
> more effectively instead of providing clues which end up being
> dead give-aways. Perhaps practice will eventually iron out these
> difficulties. After today I am feeling more positive about my teach-
> ing. (Lisa)

> My explanations could have been much clearer and better. I
> explained one aspect wrongly so I had to stop and re-explain that
> part. I felt pretty stupid making that mistake but I'm glad I realised
> I had made it fairly quickly. (Jane)

My mistakes have all contributed to the process of learning to teach ESL. I realised today I left out certain parts of my explanation so when I explain things that I want all the class to take notice of, I really have to make them stop what they are doing and give me their undivided attention. (Jane)

An aspect of teaching, for which it is difficult to prepare students anywhere but in the classroom, is the complex and unpredictable nature of the progress of lessons. Strategies for coping with the unexpected were being explored by the following students:

The main problem with my Year 8 English lesson was that it was too dependent on their having done all their homework. Most of the students had only done part. I felt at a loss especially as I didn't have any back-up material, so it was an important lesson in itself — always have something else to fall back on and don't fully depend on homework being done as a basis for a lesson. I picked up a number of smaller points in the lesson such as getting the students to read their own work rather than me. (Jane)

I felt quite stupid a few times that I could not explain simple words that I had taken for granted — that I simply had not thought about. Discussion of this class with the supervising teacher showed that I did a number of things wrong. I forgot about the girl in the corner and missed asking questions to two fairly quiet people. Also I had to stand at the front and use my voice a bit more. Actually, I know I should have pre-planned a bit more. And I thought that as a 'good class', they could settle themselves down. Oh well. Wrong! (Alice)

As has been said, the journals were dialogue journals in which teachers sometimes responded to the comments of the students. This did not happen as often as the student teachers would have wished and the students, being fairly powerless in the school, could not insist on responses but sometimes there was a comment appended to the students' entry:

Do you feel that you can actually be 'yourself' when teaching? At this stage I find I am playing the role of a teacher, rather than being able to act as myself in a classroom situation. (Christine) [To which the teacher dialogued: *Not exactly. You are your-self — but not one of them. You have to maintain a distance between the students and yourself. Be friendly and interested but they must know that you don't appreciate them asking you personal questions, etc.]*

Another student teacher was concerned about the pacing of lessons and the effect that that has on student learning:

Over the last few weeks I have noticed a definite improvement in relation to the timing of my lessons. It is amazing how short a fifty-minute lesson actually seems when everything runs smoothly and the students are enthusiastic. I am still fighting a tendency to rush through lessons and explain far too quickly rather than allowing natural pauses to occur from time to time. (Lisa)

The reflective process that produces such observations in writing is valuable for the students' observation of their professional development. The 'definite improvement' has a ring of developing confidence and the observation of the need to allow 'natural pauses' shows a maturity of thinking that some experienced teachers may not have.

The negative comments about their own teaching are obvious in all of the above comments. There must have been positive things to say about their lessons, yet they are rarely mentioned. It is true that beginning teachers make many mistakes and learn from these. But mentor teachers need to have the skill to highlight the positives and encourage the students to celebrate their successes as well as learn from their mistakes.

Developing Philosophies

The students also show developing educational philosophies which appear to be growing out of their experience in the classroom, underpinned by the theoretical talk in university seminars:

Sometimes I seriously think that John Dewey got it right — let children learn from experience. Year 7s are very convinced of their own knowledge and intelligence, which is of course far above that of the teacher. So should the teacher opt out all together and just provide the stimuli? Or should one forge ahead, against all odds, to ensure that in fact the curriculum areas are actually covered? (Ailsa)

Part of my aims as a teacher is to be able to steer students towards worthwhile learning (not necessarily academic learning). With higher retention rates there seems to be the need for a 'skills for life' strain [*sic*] in the curriculum for students who are not academic. If the service provided by teachers is not seen as useful/purposeful, the needs of many students are being overlooked. I think teachers need to see themselves as professionals and be given the scope and resources to be able to perform as such. (Christine)

I have found in general that kids are both ignorant of the world around them yet interested in it if it is presented in an interesting way. Subjects like Studies in Society are really good to teach because I believe that they do encourage students to step outside of themselves for a while, and to think. I think education should do that. (Rachel)

Discipline and Classroom Management

Discipline and classroom management are the two greatest concerns for the practising student teacher. Many of their reflections are directed to this area of the teacher's craft. It is evident from the following journal responses that survival in the classroom, involving discipline and classroom management procedures, is of great concern to these student teachers. They feel that, without a degree of order, they cannot teach and that students cannot learn:

Classroom management is such a big part of being a successful teacher — without it you are unable to teach effectively and students are unable to learn effectively. I'm always stunned at how naturally experienced teachers assume their roles as the ones 'in charge' — for me it is a conscious effort to maintain 'control'. I don't want to be authoritarian or take the fun out of learning, but it is so frustrating trying to talk over students or constantly disciplining students rather than getting on with some meaningful learning. (Christine)

Sometimes it's frustrating when hours of work preparation are thrown out the window as a result of time spent dedicated to classroom management. However, this is something I have to get used to. (Rachel)

It is unfortunate that Rachel feels that she has to get used to a situation that she knows is counter-productive. There is a sense of powerlessness in the above comment. The discourse of powerlessness is common in the 'talk' of student teachers. They are not recognised as 'proper' members of staff by anyone in the school and so often find that, as well as feeling powerless in an unruly classroom, areas such as photocopying, collecting of resource materials, knowing about meetings are closed to them. They are afraid of unwittingly doing the wrong thing 'politically' in the school. Mentor teachers have a special responsibility to 'empower' their students in these ways.

The student below is exploring possible reasons for and possible solutions to the discipline problems she is experiencing.

> I find it difficult to relate to a group as large as 29 students —
> it often seems that while your attention is drawn to one group,
> the others begin to get restless. What measures can be taken
> to get students' attention? . . . I find it difficult to gain responses
> from some students, e.g. not willing to answer questions/write
> sentences. Are some students merely at school because there
> is little alternative (not really interested) or is the topic itself of
> little interest? What types of activities would they like to do?
> (Christine)

In the following reflection, there is a growing recognition of the ability of an experienced teacher to ease up on draconian discipline methods as respect and credibility are gained, and the satisfaction that this can bring:

> [At the Language Centre] students may speak in their own language and move around freely during class. At first it seemed like a challenge to the teacher's authority but I think it means that the teacher must gain control through respect and not fear.
> (Trish)

Some students find being authoritarian in the classroom, in order to gain control, alien and abhorrent. Taking on the mantle of a disciplinarian figure goes against the image they have of themselves and often of the philosophy of life they have built up as a student. Their journals show them struggling with what they would like ideally and what the out-of-control situation seems to dictate:

> I can see what I should be doing discipline-wise in general but
> when the situation arises, it's hard to know exactly what to say

without going about it the wrong way. It seems so farcical standing up and acting in such an authoritarian manner — not when other teachers are doing it, but when I am. It comes back to practice and confidence in the classroom. I can imagine having your own classroom and knowing the children from day one would make a big difference. (Mandy)

While I don't feel uncomfortable in 'telling off' students when necessary, I'm a little unused to actually dictating how I want the class to behave. It's a matter of reminding myself that I'm in charge of the class and that I have to set the agenda for behaviour. In the next few lessons I'll try to concentrate on classroom management. (Christine)

Last lesson they [Year 11] seemed to have made up their minds not to do any work — they were disruptive and obviously disinterested [*sic*]. The few who actually wanted to follow the lesson weren't able to be heard above the others. From my point of view, I expect the students to behave according to their own sense of 'fair play', respect for others, etc. Perhaps things don't operate like that? I dislike having to keep stopping the class to keep 'order', and yet if I don't, I'm not doing my job as a person responsible for developing students' skills in language (including listening and contributing to discussion). What happens next? (Christine)

The questions being pondered above, and the statement, 'I expect the students to behave according to their own sense of fair play, respect for others . . .' show a young person having her ideals tested. Experienced teachers can judge a student teacher adversely if classroom management is weak. Mentors should be aware of the philosophical difficulties that some student teachers have with being a strong disciplinarian.

The strengthening of resolution as a discipline situation becomes desperate is seen in the following comment, but it is unfortunate that the student in her desperation reverted to a reactionary teaching style:

I lost their attention and control a few times especially when two of the boys at the front think it's great to hurl abuse at each other and everyone else. I gave them detention. The thing that struck me most was the structure of the classroom [*she does not say what it was but it must have been in groups*]. I hated it. I thought this was a main reason for disruption in the class. I think I will try the 'Neo-classical' style next time [*see Kemmis, Cole and Suggett 1983*]. I'll put the desks into lines in twos and stand at the front. (Alice)

In the following excerpt, the student teacher can be seen over-punishing in her desperation to gain control — a mistake that most experienced teachers will empathise with. It is interesting that she can see that she has made a strategic error, which, with no credit to her, turned out well.

The Year 7s went berserk! I changed the room around and separated kids. That seemed to work alright. However, the kids yell at each other and especially pick on this chubby girl (I think I'll move the name-caller further across the room.) The main problem was that I gave detention to the whole class and because we don't have Year 7 English today, most of them won't remember and won't turn up. I should have told them again near the end of the lesson and made sure they under-stood. . . . I surprised myself! Most of the kids turned up for detention but because I was a little late, the less eager ones bolted. (Alice)

The following is an interesting acknowledgment that there is a body of knowledge outside personal experience that could be a help. Courses that deal with disruptive children, or classroom management or even co-operative teaching as a management strategy, often have little relevance until the student teacher is actually in a classroom situation. Only then can they look to the 'theory' to apply it to their specific situation.

I think I need to read up on discipline techniques because they just become too rowdy and talkative sometimes. (Alice)

Solutions to discipline problems are as diverse as the students themselves. The students below appear, from their journal entries, to be working by trial-and-error as they struggle along the continuum from being 'not a teacher' to being 'a teacher':

The one aspect of the lesson that worried me was not having everyone's attention. I think I need to repeat that if I do not have every person's attention, we will practise silence during the lunch hour. (Alice)

During this *practicum* I have been able to witness some pre-ventative disciplinary techniques in action. They do seem to be effective and the use of clearly stated and displayed rules seems to be an excellent idea. In the classroom where the rules were clearly articulated and the students reminded of their respons-ibilities, I noticed that the students were better mannered and more considerate than in other classes I have encountered. (Lisa)

I think I've found the all-time answer to classroom management — learners have an attention span of ten minutes. If you have a thirty-eight minute lesson, all you need do is change learning structure three times, allowing for a period of transition and initial settling of the class. Also, it takes time to give instructions and then get them going on task. Hopefully this would make the most effective use of class time. The approximately eight minutes spent in organisation and transition are easily lost during a regular lesson plan with simply having to keep learners on task. So this is my latest tactic. I will try it out over the next few days. I think that this kind of tactic will mean that students will have to exert themselves rather than the teacher being the lone exhausted member of the classroom. (Ailsa)

The relief of the 'a-ha' experience is almost tangible! But the comment in the last sentence of the above excerpt about exhaustion was echoed throughout the journals. Student teachers find their practice teaching sessions exhausting and stressful.

Stress and Exhaustion

The stress that student teachers find themselves under is shown in the following telling comments. They show that practice teaching, when done conscientiously, is exhausting for the student teacher. This is something that a mentor teacher must take into account when putting pressure on a student teacher to complete tasks.

I feel exhausted. Each day reinforces the belief that teaching is both hard work and a lot of work. (Rachel) [To which her teacher replied, '*All teachers feel tired for most of the time, especially during peak marking times.*']

I think teaching because of the heavy emotional, mental and physical elements has a rapid burn-out rate — and I think many teachers have been teaching for too long. (Trish)

The above comment stems not only from her own exhaustion, but also from a perceptive observation of staff members and even mentor teachers. When schools are appointing mentor teachers, care should be taken to appoint teachers who have not 'burnt out'. Young student teachers find the task of practice teaching difficult enough without a negative image being projected to them by their guide and mentor.

I'm feeling disillusioned today. Tiredness is part of it most probably but I feel as if I'm struggling to do things well. (Mandy)

Throughout the duration of my practicum, I find it very difficult to sleep. When I do manage to sleep, I end up dreaming about school and classes. This nocturnal teaching is exhausting and I have often wondered whether it's an affliction common to student teachers. By the end of a three week practicum, I need days to wind down and catch up on lost sleep. (Lisa)

After preparing and delivering four lessons in one day, I find that towards the end of the day, it is more of a challenge keeping students on task than in the morning. Perhaps this is also due in part to student-teacher fatigue. (Lisa) [to which her teacher replied, '*Mental fatigue is one of our occupational hazards, I'm afraid. The first ten years or so are the worst!*']

Back to Discipline and Classroom Management

The metaphor of war and battle appears in the discourse at times, with such words as 'victory' and 'battleground':

I didn't enjoy Year 9 at all today. They've been good all week, yet for some reason they were off the planet today. I got them under control eventually, but it wasn't an easy victory. I don't like lessons that are a battleground for control. I hate having to nag and constantly pause for silence. (Rachel)

There were, however, other comments about discipline and classroom management — some showing an irrepressible humour:

I wonder if teachers will ever be in a position to treat the younger kids as humans — I guess society has to change first. Teaching younger grades tends to put a huge dent in one's self-confidence. I feel I've had to spend the whole of the day using my voice at its maximum. I feel as if I am yelling, but my supervisors tell me it is necessary. I'm using the silent, but deadly, stare at the moment. I really hate punitive measures. (Ailsa)

After attempting to supervise an exam with Year 8 English I was considering changing my degree to something incorporating homicidal mania. Thankfully my Year 8 history class rescued my sanity. I honestly did not have the psychic energy to control them if they had not been co-operative. They were angels, and for the first time this prac. I really enjoyed a class. (Ailsa)

Here [Intensive Language Centre], quite simply, teachers expect students to be punctual, polite, interested, diligent — and they are. In turn, students expect to be rewarded for this behaviour, and they are — with more interesting methods of learning, excursions, hands-on experience, new topics. (Trish)

The Supervising Teacher

Personal commitment of supervising teachers was high on the following student teacher's list of priorities. The modelling role of a supervising teacher is very important:

I'm becoming more convinced every day that teachers cannot be effective until they put themselves into everything they teach. I do not believe anyone can teach something — anything — unless they believe in it completely. Teachers must take responsibility for the example they are. A teacher must represent some standard, preferably the standard they expect from the learners. (Ailsa)

It is good to watch other teachers in action. I find that watching other teachers reinforces my belief that I am actually developing my own style. I don't find observation anywhere near as daunting as I used to. (Rachel)

Students observe their mentor teachers closely. The other side of the observation 'coin' is revealed in the following comment:

Watching experienced teachers in action exacerbates my feelings of nervousness. I feel more tense when I am teaching in front of a supervising teacher. Perhaps because I know I am being judged, I try too hard. I've noticed that I am far more relaxed when I am the only teacher present in the classroom. (Lisa)

The task of observation is integral to mentoring and supervision. Ways have to be found that are mutually comfortable for the mentor and the student teacher.

Student teachers are powerless in a school. They do not belong to the established staff, and, without care, they can be made to feel very much unwanted:

I just feel like a bit of a nuisance to my supervisors, however, two other teachers on the staff have gone out of their way to help me and encourage me . . . I'm not completely certain as to what I have to do just yet as most of my supervisors are very busy. Doubtless I will eventually find out. (Ailsa)

A surprising comment on the age of the supervising teacher came from Ailsa who seemed to be stifled by a mentor who would not allow her to take risks:

I feel it needs to be said that sometimes a young second or third year out teacher can be of greater assistance to a prac. teacher than one who has developed his/her own style and is convinced of its superiority. (Ailsa)

She goes on to say:

. . . unfortunately at this stage the student is almost totally at the supervisor's mercy. If supervisors are prepared to be paid for their services, they should be prepared to give the student an amount of freedom to experiment. Only one of my three supervisors has given me the freedom to do what I want . . . I know I could never tell my supervisor that they are cramping my style . . . I feel that this particular teacher has me in 'student' mould and thus I feel really intimidated . . . one of my supervisors is very encouraging — the youngest of them — and seems to think my ideas are working well. (Ailsa)

Mentor teachers in their working with student teachers should signal to them by the way they treat them that they see them as potential colleagues, that they value the freshness and new ideas that they bring to the classroom. They should allow them, under supervision and monitoring, to experiment and try ideas that they have brought from university. The student, on the other hand, has to realise that, in the long run, it is the pupils who will suffer if their 'experiments' do not work, and that a responsible mentor teacher cannot allow that to happen. So there is a compromise to be reached here. The student has to recognise that the mentor has a wealth of experience that will inform any cautionary measures that he/she takes. On the other hand, mentors should not be so set in their ways that they are not able to be in-serviced by the student teacher. The constant refreshment that constitutes the professional development that student teachers can bring to their supervising teachers is a very valuable aspect of mentoring. Ailsa, in the comments above seems to have a problem with having so many supervising teachers. She says at another place in her journal:

> For some reason, methods I used with extreme success on my last prac. have not appeared to be so successful this time. I wonder if it's due to my feeling slightly bewildered with having four separate supervisors and trying to give each one what they want which is basically what it comes down to a lot of the time. (Ailsa)

Other Issues

When students reflect on such issues as gender, multiculturalism, social and individual differences in the way they do in the following extracts from their journals, it can be seen that when these issues are contextualised in the school, the students recognise their importance in the teaching and learning process.

For example, students were conscious of gender issues as they reflected on what was happening in their classrooms:

> My only concern is that the girls seem to be reluctant to take any meaningful part in discussion — I feel as if I am favouring the boys by responding to them more often than the girls (either to discipline or to answer questions). Even standing to the side of the room where the boys sit seems to reinforce their dominance of the classroom. I would like to draw out/include the girls more so that they can be rewarded for participation. (Christine)

In my lessons I have tried to use a variety of approaches so as to take into consideration the differing learning styles of the students. I have tried aural, oral, visual and activity-based methods. Much to my dismay, I've noticed that in the lower grades, the boys invariably take up more of my time in the classroom than do the girls. The boys are louder, more boisterous and attention-seeking than the girls. (Lisa)

Were it not for the university's theoretical emphasis on gender differences, I feel I may have been too busy to have noticed that the boys' behaviour does influence the amount of time the teacher spends with them. (Lisa)

The contribution of social problems to the dynamics of the classroom was made evident to one student:

I thought teenage suicide only took place in the USA. I'm finding out differently these days. Broken homes, drugs, underage sex, unwanted pregnancies — this is all that young people have to come to terms with. The learning involved with school must seem so petty at times. (Ailsa)

And the effect on teaching that personal problems and circumstances can have was brought home to another:

I had a run-in with a rail official on my way to the school and that set my mood for the day. It just highlights the fact that teachers are people and because the work is so people-oriented, things which occur outside the school can't help but affect things occurring in it. (Trish)

The students were also contextualising the psychological elements of the teacher education course, and their journals show them wrestling with notions of how students learn and what affects their learning:

Consistency! Today I learnt that one of the most important aspects of being a teacher (or probably a parent) is to be consistent. Regardless of mood or energy levels or personal crises, treatment of, attitude towards and expectations of the students, the teacher must be consistent. This is especially important in the early stages of a relationship. A new class arriving only last week found their teacher quite agreeable, but this week, the same teacher with Asian flu, turned into something else. The students, not understanding this, not knowing their teacher or customs, or even knowing the language, were quite distraught at the personality change. (Trish)

I wanted to teach and this is how I imagined it to be — civilised. Not, as in previous pracs., a battle of wills. I want to be there. The students want to be there. We all want to learn. We all want to participate and offer what we can. And no one wants to dominate. It is an ideal situation. However, it means that I must be very adaptive, changing to each new situation — each new class. And they are vastly different. These classes have such different dynamics that the teacher has to be very responsive. I am surprised — and delighted — at my ability to adapt. (Trish)

I'm feeling like a run-of-the-mill non-progressive type teacher today. I spent two lessons in a row with Year 8 having to raise my voice more times than I would have liked. I think perhaps I need to rethink my lesson designs as I am inclined towards inquiry/interactive learning styles and am thus looking for class participation in discussion. This wonderful idea falls down however, in the face of a classroom filled with overactive hormones, and kids lacking the sense to cope with them. I'm quite fed up with the constant smart comments which are always loud enough to drown out the students that are doing some good work. I've never asked a student to leave the room and I really wouldn't like to, but if some of these kids don't get control of themselves, I'm seriously going to have to think up some threats. (Ailsa)

Reflection on University Preparation for Practicum

When asked to reflect on the relationship of the university-based aspects of the course and the school-based aspects, one student made the following comments:

I find practicum much more useful and pertinent than university theory. Teachers at practicum are good to talk to because they discuss things realistically, are credible, unlike a lot of the academics who focus on theory which is of no use when you're standing before a sea of strange expectant faces, wondering what to do next. (Rachel)

I feel that university has so far not assisted me during my practicum. Perhaps that is a harsh judgment. Perhaps it has helped me get this far. (Rachel)

The longer I am into the practicum the more I see the deficiencies in some of our university courses. I really think that the Dip.Ed. courses need to deal with basics, because it is basics which are needed in the classroom. (Rachel). [*to which the teacher replied, 'I agree totally with you.'*]

The following student appears to be moving out of survival mode and into autonomous practice mode. There is evidence of development, and ability to link theory and practice to achieve better practice:

In my last prac I felt the theoretical aspect of education examined at university was of little value. However, here the scope for implementing new ideas is so great it is wonderful to have a background which provides a stimulus for new ideas. (Trish)

Whereas, the student below appears still to be in survival mode:

I wish they had more practical hints about programming and lesson planning in our Dip.Ed. (Mandy)

Finally, linking in with the moves towards more of a school-base to teacher education courses, one student commented:

Dip.Ed. students should really be given more school experience as this is where real learning happens. (Jane)

And Finally

This section has listened to the voices of some student teachers as they speak through their journals. We have looked into the lived experience of these student teachers as they have endeavoured to rehearse in the classroom the theory that they have heard about in their university lectures, and then have tried to put into words the processes that are taking place in that classroom experience.

It is important for teachers who undertake to supervise or to mentor a practising student that they have some understanding of the kinds of discourses of thinking that these students have shown in the excerpts from their journals quoted above. Such journal entries can show that a disastrous lesson is not an example of incompetence or ineptness, but a learning experience, albeit a painful one. Rather than being a sign of inability or inadequacy, it can be the result of a 'run-in with a railway official on the way to school', or the result of worry over a sick mother. Mentor teachers can learn from such journals as they glimpse the world of the student teacher through the student's own eyes.

In the next chapter, we listen to both supervising teachers and practising students as they revue what the *practicum* has meant for them.

Chapter 3

The Past Role of the Teacher — Supervision as Socialisation

Barbara Field

Introduction

In the past, supervisors of pre-service teacher education students welcomed the students into the school, made sure they knew the 'geography' of the building, introduced them to the staff, told them where to buy their lunch, made sure that they had suitable accommodation and travel arrangements. They gave them a desk in the staff room and showed them where the resources for lessons were. They gave them as much or as little help as they perceived was needed for the preparation of lessons. They looked over student lesson notes before they went into class and made suggestions if they saw that there was something that could go drastically wrong. They sat in on lessons and gave them feedback on the presentation, style and content after the lesson was over. They made sure that the students did playground duty and sports duty and sometimes bus duty, and that the students were invited to staff meetings and to any staff function after school. Having done all of that, they felt that the students would become socialised into the school through experiencing these kinds of 'help'. 'Supervision' in past style was essentially seen as socialisation or enculturation into the school context.

Socialisation into Teaching

Zeichner and Gore (1990:329) define 'socialisation' as 'that process whereby the individual becomes a participating member of the society [of teachers]'. They go on to identify three main traditions of socialisation — the *functionalist*, which is rooted in the tradition of sociological positivism, holding the view that the 'society' is stable and that people are initiated and integrated into this solidarity; the *interpretive*, rooted in the tradition of social, critical thought, asking questions and seeking explanations for social phenomena; and the *critical*, in which people are seen as not only the products of the society, as the functionalists would have it, but as the creators of it.

The experience that pre-service teacher education students have had in schools, in the past, has been essentially one of *functionalist* socialisation. During their time in the school, the student-teachers were moulded by experienced supervisors to fit the particular school environment. If the student teacher and the supervising teacher held different but equally legitimate views about teaching and learning, the student was likely to acquire a 'temporary' teaching style — that of the supervising teacher — that they felt would gain them a passing grade (Duffy 1987:266). Britzman (1991:237) claims that teachers often begin the *practicum* period with 'intentions of enhancing student potential and find this intention thwarted by socially patterned routines' and that student teachers often describe their involuntary collusion with, for example, authoritative pedagogy as 'learning what not to do'. This is part of the powerlessness, discussed in the last chapter, of student teachers as they practise in a school. They are not in a position to question the *status quo* and so they adapt to it for the time.

This chapter deals with the socialising role of supervision. Chapter 4 will outline the new role of supervising/mentoring teachers — that of teacher educator. However, it has to be remembered that embedded in that new role is the traditional socialising role of the supervising teacher. It is this socialising role that is to be explored in this chapter.

In a small study carried out by Webster (1993) of the University of Melbourne with two schools undertaking to supervise practising students, the responses to questions about what constitutes 'good supervision' were oriented to caring, socialising practices. The general principles were:

- making student teachers feel one of the staff;
- making students feel welcome in the classroom;
- expecting the children to show the same behaviour towards student teachers as towards themselves;
- modelling and explaining what and why they are doing what is done;
- discussion and feedback on the student teacher's work.

This practical, house-keeping list shows the distance that separates the level of the teacher educator, that mentoring demands, from that of the role of supervisor. The role of mentor demands a much deeper treatment of the processes that are going on in the classroom than this list reveals. All of the elements of the list are necessary and important — there needs to be added to it the elements that will be discussed in Chapter 4.

What Does Supervision Mean?

A study on the supervision of practising student teachers was carried out in the North West Education Region of New South Wales, Australia, (Field 1992a). Teachers were asked what they thought 'to supervise' meant. They were asked to respond with a verb. They invariably listed positive, encouraging verbs — never harsh negative verbs. They expressed such things as encourage, assist, guide, question, praise, rescue. They even avoided verbs such as 'judge' and 'assess', even though they knew they had to write a comprehensive report on the student's practice, and grade the student on a continuum from Excellent to Unsatisfactory.

Some of the verbs collected from across the 130 participants were:

encourage	guide	observe	direct
advise	demonstrate	praise	collaborate
offer alternatives	oversee	monitor	be available
be a role model	help/assist	rescue	motivate
share	suggest	be a counsellor	tend/nurture

set limits to risk while allowing risk-taking to occur
make aware of school routines

In the above list of verbs and expressions, one of the discourses that comes through strongly in the 'talk' of teachers about supervision is that of empowering. There is a nurturing and enculturating discourse that runs through the above verbs. Teachers believe that the 'babes' in the profession, the neophytes, have to be helped and assisted into the ways that the supervising teacher knows of being a teacher. The teachers' responses in this project indicate that supervising teachers are usually very kind to student teachers.

In a study in the USA, a teacher defined her supervisory role in terms of 'emotional support and practical suggestions. Her job [was] to be there, ready to listen and give counsel' (Feiman-Nemser and Parker 1992:2), and again: 'The support teachers bring resources and materials to new teachers. They offer instructional assistance related to content and methodology. They give a lot of emotional support through empathetic listening and sharing experiences . . .' (Feiman-Nemser and Parker 1992:5).

Even though there was this consistent discourse of caring in the New South Wales study, there was always the caveat that supervising teachers had to be honest. They do not want to back away from their responsibilities to tell the student the truth about their practice, if it is not adequate. But they want to have the skill to be able to do this in as positive a way as possible. They want the skill to be able to walk the tightrope between the truth and diplomacy.

There are obviously conflicting discourses such as this in the minds of thoughtful supervisors of practice teaching under the scheme of teacher education where only about 25 per cent of course time is spent in schools, and time is short for the development of relationships. Teachers recorded verbs such as negotiate, collaborate, be patient, but, on the other hand, they listed be honest, set guidelines, criticise constructively. So there are tensions in the practice teaching supervision role. There is a wish and a need to be nurturing and empowering to the student but also a realisation that, in the long run, the role of judge and assessor cannot be avoided.

The teachers know that the student teachers perceive the advising role as a telling /directing role. Student teachers know that the supervising teacher who is being encouraging and positive to them will be taking into account the shortcomings under discussion when the report is written. They will be judging how much notice the student teacher has taken of the advice given. This tension between the roles of guide and mentor on the one hand, and judge and jury on the other is evident in responses.

In a study of the meetings between supervisor and student teacher, Kagan and Albertson (1987:53) analysed the discourses and found the following to be the most common elements in the conversations:

- perceived problems or concerns;
- what the student is doing correctly;
- what the student is doing incorrectly;
- the student teacher's mastery of content;
- the student teacher's rapport with pupils;
- preparation of lessons;
- 'housekeeping' matters such as scheduling observations;
- personal characteristics such as voice, appearance.

The above list shows how conferencing under the old system of supervision needed only to concentrate on the immediate practical concerns of the student teacher. The new tasks of mentors will include, as well as these immediate concerns, more searching work on areas such as which beliefs about education are driving a particular way of teaching; alternatives to these beliefs; what social and community issues are affecting the teaching/learning possibilities in the classroom. Teachers will be trained in these new skills by programs developed jointly by both schools and universities (see Chapters 5–8).

Conflicting Philosophies

Student teachers sometimes find that the school in which they are placed for *practicum* has a philosophy of teaching and learning that runs counter to the way they see their own role as a facilitator of learning. It is then that the socialising process by a strong teacher can cause friction. A mature-age student wrote in a *post-practicum* survey on supervising teachers:

> She only had one way of teaching and that was EXACTLY how she expected me to do it. Any suggestion I made (i.e., painting, cooking, etc.) was too messy so we couldn't do them. This was insisted upon to the degree that she dictated, step-by-step, the lesson and how it was to be done. If I did exactly what she did I was fine. I had to reproduce her type of lesson. I think she thought she was doing the right thing. I am concerned that a young person could have her as a supervisor and think that this was the right way to teach. After all, the supervisor is the one who is the example to follow.

The strength of the socialising that is taking place here does not negate the caring, nurturing discourse. The student teacher admits that the teacher is certain that she is doing the best for the student teacher. But the teacher is also determined that her ways will be taken up in the person of this new teacher. The teacher perceives that the stability of the school 'society' hinges on the continuation of her teaching style.

Conflict was mentioned only once by teachers in the New South Wales study and then only in passing. Teachers seem not to anticipate that there will be a clash of personalities. Only one teacher in the study talked openly about having had a student that she just could not get on with. She had immediately, for the sake of the student, asked that he be transferred to another supervising teacher. Perhaps the reason for the supervising teachers' not perceiving the conflict is, as has been said, that student teachers keep their thoughts to themselves because of the need to gain a passing grade. It is the experience of those who organise the practice teaching session for many students that the clash of personalities occurs more often than would be apparent from the responses in the study. The comment by the student teacher above was written in a *post-practicum* survey for the university, not said to the teacher. Perhaps some skills in conflict resolution would not go astray. In a socialisation process where the stability of the school society is being guarded by supervising teachers, integrating and initiating students into this society can lead to conflict.

Professional Development of Mentors through Supervision

Despite the report from the student quoted above, it was interesting to note that, in the New South Wales study into the supervisory process, most teachers said that they valued the fact that student teachers often have skills that they themselves do not have. The two-way interchange is valued by the teachers. If a student can train the brass section of the band, that is a plus. One teacher said that the pupils at her school still played a sports game that a student had taught them two years ago. Another teacher said she was still using the unit of work her student had prepared for a *practicum* session some years ago. A music teacher was delighted with the work her student teacher had done with her classes on music and computers — areas that she did not feel competent to deal with. If these examples were given by teachers in the system where only 25 per cent of the teacher education course was taken up by the *practicum,* how much more would the expertise of student teachers be used in a more school-based system of teacher education.

Communication and Conferencing

Communication and conferencing skills are seen as important supervision skills by supervising teachers. In the workshops in the New South Wales study, teachers brainstormed what people mean by communication skills and came up with many aspects of the supervising role in reply to the question, 'What are some of the ways of communicating/conferencing effectively?'

- be a good listener;
- try not to 'tell';
- ask 'open' questions;
- allow time for thinking and reflecting before answering;
- write down what is said — for reference;
- have set guidelines/parameters;
- negotiate the guidelines and expectations;
- be open and flexible adopt others' ideas;
- be assertive not aggressive;
- recognise the other's rights;
- be honest — don't hedge;
- show care, concern;
- respect and value the other's opinions;
- have a set time that cannot be interrupted;
- recognise that it is a two-way process;
- don't overload with information;

In the above responses, emphasis is given by supervising teachers to the importance of making time for the supervising teacher and student teacher to talk with and listen to each other. There was a conscience about this among the committed group of teachers in the New South Wales study. They talked a lot about the busy-ness of the school day and how they realised they had to be disciplined about arranging times for conferencing with the student, and keeping to those times. In the new scheme of mentoring, the *practicum* has to be much more structured and time is built in for conferencing, whereas it was done 'on the run' in the past. Some of the students in a recent *post-practicum* survey actually complained about the busy-ness of their supervising teachers and they claimed that teachers who had many responsibilities should not be involved in the time-consuming task of supervision as well:

> My teacher was involved in many other activities within and outside the school which seemed to limit the time in which I could speak to her.

> My supervisor was a senior teacher and was out of the room a good deal. He did not see a lot of my teaching and did not evaluate many lessons.

> She wasn't there for help.

Partington (1982:270) in a study of PGCE students and their supervising teachers at Nottingham University found that there was a 'flurry of advice and help at the beginning' of the *practicum* followed by a tapering off. Partington suggests that 'perhaps colleagues in the school felt that they had no more to offer from which their student might benefit'. He also says: 'Meetings with Miss X were usually brief, in between lessons, and interrupted by the usual necessity to be somewhere else with a responsibility.' This pin-points exactly the problem of the students above. It is something that teachers in the role of supervisor could do, but when they take on the deeper, heavier load of mentor, they will not be able to do. When student teachers are in schools for two-thirds of their courses, conferencing sessions between mentor and student, which will become teacher education sessions, will have to be time-tabled. (see Chapter 4 and Chapters 5–8 for ways in which individual university/school partnerships are working this out.)

Teachers in the New South Wales study also showed that they realise that, in the conferencing sessions, they should not overload the student with information or advice, but ask open-ended questions so that the student can reflect. The temptation, at the end of a lesson, is for the teacher to tell the student what he or she could have done to make the lesson more successful, instead of asking the student to critique his/her own practice. The teachers in the study wanted written and spoken communication of opinions and reflections by both the teacher and the student — a two-way process. The study using dialogue journals with practising students came some way to achieving this kind of open and frank communication. (See Chapter 2).

Help

In the New South Wales study, as the participants made their way towards listing some skills and competencies needed for the supervision of *practicum*, they discussed how they could intervene in the process of the student-teacher's moving from 'not-a-teacher' to 'a teacher' so that they helped and did not maim. The following list of suggestions is what the workshop groups developed in answer to the stimulus: 'Let us consider carefully what help means in the supervisory process. How can we, as teachers, intervene in the necessary struggle of the student to become a teacher?'

- have a pre-lesson conference for every lesson;
- have a post-lesson conference for every lesson;
- give a repertoire of strategies for class management;
- help the students organise their time;

- help them pace the lessons and the day;
- help them sequence material logically;
- lift their motivation if necessary;
- direct them to resources;
- let them experiment;
- demonstrate techniques to them;
- emphasise the craft of teaching as well as the art;
- teach them to preview materials, e.g. videos;
- tell them about mannerisms, speech defects;
- leave them alone in the classroom occasionally;
- give them a range of abilities, lessons, etc.

There were animated discussions about whether it is part of the job of the supervising teacher to tell students about such things as their mannerisms, their inappropriate dress, their smell or their speech impediments. Teachers felt that these things should be dealt with at university. They were embarrassed about having to make such personal comments to students. It was a skill that they felt that they needed but didn't really want to acquire. Yet it is a very important aspect of the socialisation of students into the mores of the profession.

Motives for Supervision

Another point for reflection in the New South Wales workshops was the question, 'Why do I take a student teacher to supervise?' There were many and varied responses to this ranging from, 'for the money', to, 'because someone once did it for me.' The altruistic, positive, professional reasons far outweighed the self-centred reasons, although the teachers were honest enough and relaxed enough to put down such reasons as, 'it looks good on the *c.v.*' and, 'because I was told to,' and, 'it's an ego trip'. The university came in for some brickbats such as, 'I realise the limitations of their academic courses', but it also came in for some bouquets: 'keeps you in touch with uni's views and happenings', and 'to be kept up to date with the new methodology'.

Professional development for themselves was high on the teachers' list of reasons for supervising the *practicum*. 'I learn from the student', 'it focuses my own teaching', 'reflective — helps you step back from what you are doing' 'to rejuvenate, re-evaluate my ideas.' This aspect of supervision/mentoring is dealt with in detail in the concluding chapter. Teachers were embarrassed about saying that they felt that they had something to offer — but, when they were encouraged, they did say such things as: 'I can model good teaching'; 'I've got something to offer'; 'passing on experience'.

There was a 'company'/ 'collegiality' discourse coming through in some of the responses that seemed to point to the loneliness that some teachers can feel in their classrooms, especially in small, isolated schools: 'to take part in a two-way exchange of ideas'; 'gives the opportunity for team teaching'; 'to use student's expertise. I always learn something from them'.

A sense of professional obligation was obvious in some responses: 'a sense of duty'; 'to help the university'; 'to promote teaching as a profession'. Teachers acknowledge that if they want to influence the standard and quality of young teachers coming into the profession, they have to be prepared to take part in the training of those students. It adds to their work load, but they believe it is necessary. The nurturing discourse was obvious in such responses as: 'to contribute to a student's development'; 'it can benefit the children'; 'students need the practical experience'; 'past memories of terror'; 'to give student teachers better help than I received'. Teachers think first of their own classes and many acknowledge that having a student in the classroom adds a dimension that can only be beneficial. They also think that if they accept a student and treat them kindly, it could save them from being treated unkindly by another teacher. Many experienced teachers had memories of unhappy practice teaching sessions.

I have said that supervision, in the past, has been a process of the socialisation of student teachers into the mores of a school life. It is interesting, then, that, in the above responses, when teachers were outlining what it is they do in supervision, they do not articulate exactly that they are in a process of socialising the students into the *status quo*. It is apparent from what they say that this socialisation process is going on, but it seems it is not perceived as such by teachers.

Skills and Competencies for Supervising Teachers

Finally, a tentative list of skills and competencies for the supervision of practising students was compiled by the participants in the New South Wales study:

> A supervising teacher should be able to:
>   be articulate about teaching practices;
>   analyse what is happening in a lesson;
>   tread the line between diplomacy and truth;

empower student-teachers;
model good practice;
recognise signs of stress;
recognise what is not remediable;
be a good listener.

A supervising teacher should have the skills of:
questioning;
interviewing/conferencing;
organising.

These skills and competencies are those of supervision and they will all still be necessary in the broader task now being asked of teachers in schools when they take on the role of mentor. Supervision skills are still basic to the whole role of mentoring. There are, however, new skills and competencies needed for the mentoring role that have to be added to the supervision skills. These will be dealt with in Chapter 4.

What Do the Student Teachers Say?

The preceding data were collected from teachers who have been in the supervisory role in schools for student teachers. Teachers themselves were talking about what they see as their role.

In the second workshop in the New South Wales study, practising student-teachers were present. They surprised the teachers with their ability to articulate what they thought about the supervision process. The comments below from a different group of students from the ones writing in Chapter 2, add to the data from the reflective journals in that chapter. The students were asked to relate to the teachers what they perceived as helpful and unhelpful supervisory practices. (It should be noted that none of the students present was being supervised by any of the teachers present, so they felt free to say what they felt.)

. . . the most helpful supervisory practices for student teachers in their schools.

- visiting the school before the *practicum* begins for briefing;
- being allowed to observe classes before teaching;
- being given immediate feedback on lessons;
- being given both written and spoken feedback;
- being left to manage the class by yourself sometimes;
- suggesting and providing resources;

- being treated like a colleague/member of staff/feeling welcome;
- being given advice on alternative strategies;
- observing other teachers in school;
- being given some responsibility in the school;
- having a desk set up ready;
- having name tags for pupils.

... the most un-helpful supervisory practices for student-teachers in their schools.

- teacher intervening in discipline matters;
- being corrected in front of the class;
- not being (or feeling) trusted;
- being given the lessons to do that the teacher doesn't like;
- teachers being too set in their ways;
- feeling segregated (not part of staff);
- having problems with clerical staff;
- teachers thinking they are on holidays during the practicum;
- being introduced to class as a 'trainee teacher';
- being used as casual relief;
- being held to unrealistic expectations. ('I'm only in First Year!')

Student teachers want honest feedback on their shortcomings. One unhelpful practice cited by a student teacher was a teacher's saying to her, 'You have no faults.' She felt that the teacher was either not being honest or not being very analytical. Another student commented that her teacher told her that, 'Every aspect was great and did not tell [her] how to improve'.

A common complaint was that some teachers do not give enough helpful feedback. Student teachers said such things as:

No feedback — which I needed in order to improve.

Not discussing my lessons with me. She was not even in the room to see me teach. I only had two lesson reports written out for me.

My teacher was too laid back and didn't mind what I did. I would have preferred to have more guidance.

Pre- and post-lesson conferences are seen as essential by the students, and often, time is not organised for them. Student teachers are also concerned that they be seen as colleagues in the school and that they not be introduced to the pupils in a way that makes them feel inferior. Some found that the orientation to the school, its staff and its policies and rules, had not been not very thoughtfully done, and they felt like strangers. They also wanted the teacher to be flexible and to allow them to experiment. They did not want to be exploited as free labour in the school, especially if a teacher was away sick. They felt that many teachers should learn the skills of intervening in a class situation in a way that does not make the student feel marginalised. It was helpful for the students to have been given some information about the class or classes they were to teach before the *practicum*. This last problem does not arise so much now in England, because students are in their schools for much longer periods, but in Australia, where the four-week block practice is often the only practice, students sometimes arrive at their school with little or no introduction.

Some of the comments that students made on the shortcomings of their supervisors are informative:

> My teacher made me feel like an incompetent young fool and put the blame on me for everything that happened to me and it wasn't helpful at all.

When asked what aspect of their *practicum* weakened their commitment to teaching, such replies as the following were not uncommon:

> A lot of the staff were very unwelcoming and made me feel in the way.

> My teacher didn't like me trying new things and when I did she would criticise me if it wasn't the way she would have done it. (Even if it was good).

> I found that my class couldn't be controlled by their own teacher and yet she expected me always to be in control.

> It's hard when a teacher asks: 'Why are you becoming a teacher? It's a dead end job.'

> I do not want to end up like some of the disgruntled teachers I saw on prac.

> The teacher who was supervising me did not allow me to do many lessons. She continually interrupted me and was late looking at my lesson plans and doing my reports. She also did not give me a lot of resources as I left as some of my friends' supervising teachers did.

Usually, in the student teacher/supervisor relationship, it is the supervisor who knows and the student teacher who learns. The student teacher is one who is being socialised into the community of teachers. Students, generally, view the *practicum* as the most important part of their pre-service education, seeing it as practical, satisfying and realistic.

Many studies indicate that co-operating teachers have the primary influence over the learning of student-teachers, even to the extent of negating what the students have learned from their college courses when it runs contrary to the judgments of co-operating teachers. (Emans 1983:14)

It is interesting to see what skills and attributes students themselves valued most in their supervising teacher. Students responding in the New South Wales study reported here made the following comments about their supervising teachers when asked what aspects of their *practicum* had strengthened their commitment to teaching:

- seeing how involved teachers are in their students' lives;
- having the support from other teachers;
- having an excellent teacher to learn from;
- having feedback from the teacher was helpful in building my confidence;
- having the positive reinforcement given to me by my teacher;
- having a teacher who was willing to help me learn as much as I could;
- having a teacher was very enthusiastic and enjoyed teaching.

These responses show how closely the student teachers were observing their supervising teacher. However not all of the strong influence of the supervising teachers, and teachers in general, was positive. When asked what aspects of the *practicum* weakened their commitment to teaching, some students responded:

- my supervisor not treating me as an equal friend;
- I do not want to end up like some of the teachers I saw on prac;
- the fact that there were teachers in the school who hated their job;
- constantly being given negative comments by my supervising teacher;
- seeing a lack of commitment and enthusiasm from older staff.

One of the issues coming through is the power that the supervising teacher has over the student teacher. Student teachers are powerless against the forces socialising them into the school context. These forces are reproductive rather than reconstructive. The school system reproduces itself by initiating its neophyte teachers into the system and often by getting them to surrender their autonomy and independence of thought. The university contribution to the course has tried in the past to help students to critique this process. Students at university are encouraged to question and reflect on the school context, whereas teachers who are immersed in the context often find it difficult to think objectively about it. It would seem, therefore, that there is a valuable task for university departments of education to carry out here.

Practicum Problems from the Past

Turney (1993) speaking at the National Practicum Conference in Sydney at Macquarie University, identified seven interrelated problem areas that have been associated with the *practicum* in the past. It is helpful to examine these, as the *practicum* is undergoing a transformation to see if the problems cannot be redressed under the new system.

1 There is often a disjunction between the aims stated by the university for the student teacher's practical experience in schools, and what actually happens in the *practicum*. That is, there is a gap between the ideals and the experience.
2 Often the stated aims and therefore the contingent experiences of the *practicum* are too narrow, thus limiting the experiences of the student teacher.
3 Often the classroom experiences are left to the whim of the supervising teacher and this can lead to an haphazardness and a kind of 'lottery' element in the choice of site for students' practice teaching experience.
4 The supervising teacher's influence can sometimes be counterproductive, if they teach an authoritarian, control-centred, conservative, even reactionary and backward-looking approach to classroom practice.
5 The blocks of *practicum* that we are used to are not always time-efficient in that it is not all spent purposefully and productively. In a three week block of *practicum*, it takes the student teacher at least a week to be oriented to the school. Sometimes

student teachers are left too much to their own devices. Not all of their time is taken up in teaching or observation and not all of their teaching is supervised. It could be seen as a waste of the resources, especially in money, that the university puts into it.

6 Because students can be given only one or two contexts in which to practice, they are inevitably inadequately prepared for the wide-ranging possibilities in the teaching arena.

7 Because there has been no systematic curriculum of practice teaching, we cannot demonstrate to university authorities in this time of recession that the money is being well-spent.

If the system is to change in Australia, as it has in England, it would be worthwhile to address these problem areas while reorganising and re-thinking the *practicum*.

A *Practicum* Curriculum

In the light of the above, Turney suggests that we need a *practicum* curriculum. We need, he claims, sets of specified student experiences that counter each of the problems above. We need a *practicum* curriculum that is:

- purposeful and soundly based;
- comprehensive;
- systematic;
- positive;
- efficient;
- adequate;
- demonstrably valuable.

A 'curriculum of *practicum*' that follows the above criteria and is based on the competencies identified in Chapter 1 as being needed by beginning teachers, should then become the basis for the teacher education course, and the rest of the program should be rearranged and re-packaged into courses to deliver such a curriculum. It is indisputable that the quality of the newly-qualified teacher depends at least in part on the quality of the practical experience that students have in schools. The University of Manchester, in its partnership program, has instituted such a 'Training Curriculum' (see Chapter 5).

The transformation of students from being 'not-a-teacher' to being 'a-teacher' is a very important process of becoming. This takes place in both the university, where they are encouraged to reflect on teaching issues from a distance, and in the dynamic contexts of schools where they encounter and deal with the complex and varied range of responsibilities, where they learn to respond to unexpected and unpredicted situations and where they learn the serious consequences of their actions in children's lives. It cannot be denied that this indicates a need for a more serious consideration of a 'curriculum' for *practicum*. We need, in this time of change for teacher education, to establish a knowledge base for teacher education in line with the generic skills and competencies that have been identified. We need to recognise that there is often — too often — a disjunction between what happens in schools during a *practicum* and what is taught in the teacher education program in HEIs. In the past they have often operated virtually independently, and often they were in conflict with each other. What we have asked of both students and supervising teachers has been meagre, often diverse, and too often trivial. This will change as teachers in school are made responsible for more of the teacher education course.

In Conclusion

In the past, both universities and schools have had their separate roles in the preparation of pre-service teacher education students. On both sides of the partnership there was no need for much of an understanding of what the other professionals in the teacher education program did. Now, the situation has changed dramatically in England and is changing in Australia, and there is a great need for a closer partnership between schools and universities and for the relationships within that partnership to be explored. As teacher education becomes more school-based, and so as more of the responsibility for all of the aspects of teacher education, not just the socialising aspects, fall to the classroom teacher, so there is a need for the task of the supervising teacher to be revised. This new mentoring role for teachers is considered in Chapter 4.

The New Role of the Teacher — Mentoring

Barbara Field

From Supervisor to Teacher Educator

In the past in England and Wales, and still in Australia, only about 25 per cent of the initial teacher education course has been conducted by way of *practicum* in schools. The main part of the course was conducted in universities where students learnt about how to teach. They learnt amongst other subjects, the sociology, the psychology and the philosophy of education and they learnt the theory of teaching particular subjects. They were then expected to make the connection of this information that they were given at university with the classrooms in which they were practising. The supervising teachers, as has been seen in Chapter 3, saw their task as socialising the student into the profession. The teacher education areas mentioned above were dealt with only incidentally by school teachers. Traditionally, the term 'teacher educator' has applied only to tertiary staff.

Some teacher educators are worried that making initial teacher education more school-based will result in a return to an 'apprenticeship' model of teaching. The kaleidoscope of knowledge and skills that teacher education encompasses is much more, they claim, than can be achieved by 'sitting by Nellie', no matter how good a teacher Nellie is. If the *practicum* is to be more than an apprenticeship, if teaching is more than a skilled trade, then provision has to be made in schools, in initial teacher education programs, for the relationship of theory and practice to be recognised. With an initial teacher education program that is two-thirds school-based, provision has to be made in the school's side of the partnership as well as in the university's side, for the theory/ practice link to be made. If this is not done, schools will continue to do the same as they have done in the past but, because of the increased time, will do 'more of the same'. Because of their reduced time with students, universities will do less of what they once did, and there will be a section of the program that will fall through the crack between the two. Allocating students to schools for longer periods for practice teaching should not be an exercise in gaining 'more of the same'. What is needed is 'more with a difference'. And that difference is the difference between mentoring and old-style supervision. Professional action by practising student teachers is the outcome sought by the practice teaching program. Classroom experience in longer periods of time will not necessarily deliver this. It is not the quantity but the quality of the program that is important.

The *practicum* must now become a systematic programmed teaching of all aspects of classroom teaching, not only a socialisation into the school 'society' and into the technical and craft skills needed for survival in the classroom. Because the time that students now spend in university is so limited, schools must teach some of the areas that were once thought the province of the university. Students will need to gain, in school, rather than, or as well as, in university, a knowledge of the social, psychological and philosophical underpinnings of the teaching and learning practices and processes that are going on there. They need to gain, from mentor teachers and the program organised for them in schools, an understanding of the organisation and management of the whole curriculum. They also must develop, through the school-based program, an ability to identify a personal philosophy of education that will work within the provisions and the constraints of the school context in which they find themselves. All of this was once dealt with at university, while the 'apprenticeship' skills and the socialisation into teaching were dealt with in the school.

Supervising teachers have always helped their student teachers to develop survival skills and tricks of the 'trade'. They have always taught student teachers how to plan and deliver curriculum material, and how to act as professional members of the school staff. But now that the larger proportion of the teacher education course is being delegated to schools, they need to be able to articulate to student teachers reasons for actions and behaviours in schools and to seek to explain what is happening in the teaching/learning process. Students should be permitted to ask questions and should be allowed a degree of autonomy and independence to make up their own minds on issues of belief about education, in order to avoid an apprenticeship model of teacher education. Placing more of teacher education into schools is not a looking back to an old model. It is not a reversal, but a shift in site and emphasis (Edwards 1992:2). It is indeed a *metanoia* — a transformation. It is a forward looking move to improve teacher education.

Definitions of Mentoring

The word 'mentor' needs some explanation. It connotes wisdom and antiquity from the story of Mentor and Odysseus and Telemachus. Mentor, left in charge of Odysseus' household while Odysseus went off to the Trojan War, was essentially a surrogate father and so had to personify the kingly quality of wisdom (Smith and Alred 1993:103). He had to be a father figure, a teacher, a role model, an approachable counsellor, a trusted adviser, a challenger, and an encourager to young Telemachus (Carruthers 1993:9). So, from the mythology, a mentor would appear to need qualities of leadership and wisdom, as well as skills and knowledge.

Chris Husbands (see Chapter 7) wrote in a letter, '*Mentor* is very much the "in" word but I really do not like it. It creates all sorts of notions of dependency, and the derivation from Greek mythology is not really very helpful . . . however, the term is widely accepted.' The reader can see from Husbands' chapter that in his action research processes in the University of East Anglia, he is committed to co-dependence and co-operation. Others would agree with him that the process of mentoring should be interdependent, dynamic and mutual as can be seen from the Carmin definition below. But Carmin does not balk at the word mentor.

In the book *The Return of the Mentor*, the various authors explore what the concept of mentor means in different work contexts such as hospitals, factories and schools. The book is helpful for those interested in the process of mentoring. There are useful definitions in the first chapter, 'The principles and practice of mentoring', (Carruthers 1993). One of these — Carmin's definition of mentoring — is worth quoting here in full in order to create a mind-set for this discussion of what mentoring can mean in the new setting of school-based teacher education:

> Mentoring is a complex, interactive process, occurring between individuals of differing levels of experience and expertise which incorporates interpersonal or psychosocial development, career and/or educational development, and socialisation functions into the relationship . . . To the extent that the parameters of mutuality and compatibility exist in the relationship, the potential outcomes of respect, professionalism, collegiality, and role fulfilment will result. Further, the mentoring process occurs in a dynamic relationship within a given milieu. (Carruthers 1993: 10–11)

Reflection in Mentoring

One of the skills that mentor teachers must gain is that of being able to articulate such areas of educational knowledge as their philosophy of education. This is the process of reflection. 'Reflection' is one of the buzz words in teacher education today, but it is usually used of the student teacher's reflecting on what has happened in the classroom during lessons. It is an equally important process for the experienced teacher to learn. Reflection requires the ability to articulate thoughts. As has been said (p. 28), it requires a meta-cognition — a knowing about knowing. Reflection allows a student teacher to learn and grow and change performance from one teaching episode to the next. In Chapter 2, students were reflecting on their practice as they wrote their dialogue journals. They were showing that they were beginning to know what they knew about teaching. However, they found it difficult to get their teachers to dialogue with them. Their teachers were not used to putting thoughts on their practice into words on paper.

David Frost (1993:140) lists what he believes to be the purposes of the high level reflection required of teachers and student teachers. Reflection should enable the teacher and the student teacher:

- to assess his or her own skills and to improve on them;
- to evaluate the chosen teaching strategies and materials in terms of their appropriateness;
- to question the values embedded in those practices and proceed to challenge the aims and goals of education;
- to continue to examine and clarify their personal values and beliefs about society and pedagogy;
- to theorise about the context of their pedagogical practice — that is, to try to develop explanations about the pupils, the interactions in the classroom, and about the processes of teaching and learning;
- to examine the adequacy of theories about pedagogical contexts and processes and develop a critique of them.

In this process of examining practice through reflection, teacher education in schools now is not only focused on the acquisition of classroom teaching skills, but also should teach students and mentor teachers how to analyse and question aspects of school life such as pastoral care, the effects of gender and race on classroom and school interactions, special education for individual needs and the different ways people learn. It has always been the intention in university education classes that students be challenged with different ways of looking at education. They have then learnt, in their school experience, to measure the coherence and accuracy of what they have been taught at university against the school and classroom context. They have had to work out, in the real world of the school, the justifiability and consequences of believing what they do about the whys and hows of the curriculum. It is this interrogating of practice and challenging of ideas and ideals that must not be lost in the busy-ness of a school program. Now that teacher education is being based more in schools, ways of thinking that have been encouraged at university in the past — the questioning, the posing of alternatives, the challenging of the *status quo* — must still go on. It is the task now of the mentor teacher, in partnership with the university, to encourage students to question and challenge. Feiman-Nemser and Parker write:

> the promise of mentoring lies not in its contribution to novices' emotional well-being or survival, but in its capacity to foster an inquiring stance towards teaching and a commitment to developing shared standards for judging good practice (1992:2)

There is a very real danger of these elements of the teacher education course being lost if teachers continue to perceive their task as only that of caring and nurturing. There is a distinction between social support that puts newcomers at ease and professional support that advances knowledge and practice. Dobbins and Walsey (1992) workshopped with supervising teachers the concept of teachers as teacher educators and used the following statement as a basis for the discussion:

> Just as becoming a classroom teacher involves making a transition from being a student to being a professional, so becoming a mentor involves making a transition from classroom teacher to teacher educator (1992:7)

It is this transition, and the transition from an old-style supervisor, that is under discussion in this chapter. In order for school-based teacher education to work, teachers have to take on themselves some of the tasks of teacher education that were not included in the supervisory role in the past.

The following is an example of perceptive reflection on classroom process and practice:

> A student teacher arrived at university at the beginning of his teacher education course. He had just spent a week of

observation in a school. He had studied no education theory at the time. He reported to his tutorial group that in the school, the junior high students were able to learn with independent learning techniques. Their work had been divided into manageable modules and they were making their way through these at their own pace, with obvious enjoyment and commitment, with the help of teachers and student teachers. The emphasis was on learning.

On the other hand, the senior high students who were preparing for their university entrance had had to leave that kind of learning behind them and had to sit through lectures and transmission-type teaching in order to cover the set curriculum for a public examination. The joy had gone out of their learning. It had become a chore.

Here a student teacher is reflecting on two processes in the school. He observed the commitment and progress of the junior students as they seemingly felt in control of their own learning, and compared that with the apparent indifference and inattention of the senior students who were being talked at and lectured to. He showed a grasp of this theoretical issue before any attempt had been made to characterise to him different teaching and learning styles. He had intuitively discerned a radical difference.

The Structure of Mentoring Schemes

The change from university-based to school-based teacher education has necessitated radical change in the structure of teacher education courses in England. In this chapter, the way the school-based teacher education system is working in England will be discussed in general. Four examples of specific schemes are included in Chapters 5–8.

In general, then, in the one-third of the time of the PGCE course allowed to universities, the students study two broad areas: general curriculum issues (also known as Whole School Issues), which cover, in part, what used to be known as the psychology, philosophy and sociology of education; and the specific curriculum areas which cover subject methods. In the first of these, the general curriculum studies, the terms of 'psychology', 'philosophy' and 'sociology' are usually avoided, but whatever the course is called it deals with the way children learn and their individual differences; the ways of thinking and believing about education; and the reasons for social interactions in the classroom.

In school-based teacher education, the mentor is responsible for making overt the theory in relation to school practice. For example, the mentor might ask student teachers to critique the teaching/learning styles observable in the school, and to draw some conclusions from their observations. One of the differences between mentoring and supervision is that now time has to be found in the school day for this kind of active, organised teaching of student teachers. The program has to be structured and systematic, and not done 'on the run' as it sometimes has been in the context of *practicum* 'supervision'. Mentor teachers have to ensure that time is given in the students' program of work in the school to the areas of so-called educational theory such as the one illustrated above about different teaching/learning styles. The time that the Higher Education Institution has to devote to these issues is lessening. It is necessary now to have a combined program, both school- and university-based. Mentors need to know exactly how the school experiences of the student teachers fit in with the course being delivered by the university. Each side of the partnership between school and university must build on the work of the other. The elements of the course will be jointly developed and so the course will be interrelated and jointly taught. Such a pre-service course, planned jointly between the Higher Education Institutions and the schools, will exemplify real partnership. Teachers who are to be mentors in schools should feel comfortable in the knowledge that what they are teaching student teachers complements the work of their colleagues in the university. So the planning of the course is vital. If this collaborative planning does not happen, the two elements of the course could be, at best, independent of each other, and, at worst, in conflict with each other. Chapters 5–8 show four exemplary working models of this kind of partnership organisation.

The importance of this partnership relationship is outlined in a letter to schools from The University of Leeds, where the role of the school in the school-based teacher education program was stated as follows:

Partner schools . . . provide the essential specific contexts in which students are supported in developing and rehearsing professional skills and qualities in order to become well-informed and reflective teachers.

On the other hand, the university provides the students with a physical venue in which they can meet, apart from the school, to compare and contrast experiences. The university will also work with the school in providing the theoretical framework from which students can develop a critical understanding of the schools and classrooms in which they work, and of the experiences which they have while practising their skills. Students are given the opportunity to incorporate research findings into their developing understandings of the teaching/learning process. They can discuss their research knowledge with their mentors so that the *practicum* becomes a two-way process of learning, where student teachers learn to teach from their mentors and the mentors are in-serviced by the student teachers bringing their new ideas into the school.

In the serial practice sections of the year (see Figure 4), the partnership between school and university can be most obvious. In the same week that the university tutor is dealing with, for example, classroom management theory in the general education strand of the course, the school can contextualise that theory in the classroom by demonstration and observation. In the same week that the university methods tutor is dealing with a specific subject area — for example, in English, the teaching of poetry — the school can contextualise that, too, in the classroom. The work that the student teachers do at the university in the two or three days of lectures, is dove-tailed into the work that they do in the school in the other two or three days. It is essential that both the teacher and the university tutor know what the other is teaching. This is the essence of the true partnership. Instead of students being left to make what sense they can of the relationship between what they learn at the university and what they learn in the practical world of the classroom, the connections are structured into the course. There is a logical sequence and a continuity that were not possible when the *practicum* was simply an adjunct to university studies.

The mentor will have a structured, systematic serial practice program, developed in co-ordination with university tutors. Across England there are examples of committed school mentors constructing programs of in-school seminars on teacher education topics that are linked with the classroom practice of the student teachers. At a school in Southampton, for instance, a Principal has taken on herself the task of organising the 'curriculum' for her ten student teachers. She has a ten-week program of seminars — one each week — run by various experts on the school staff and linked in with the university and classroom experience of the students. She has one session on classroom management, for example, where she takes the students to an empty classroom and asks them to comment on the arrangement of the room and its connection to potential classroom management problems. The student teachers reflect on the arrangement of the furniture, the lighting, the placing of the waste paper basket, the bareness of the walls, the lack of space, the lack of carpet on the floor and so on. The discussion is lively and the student teachers learn a great deal. She has another session where a disruptive child is questioned about his/her behaviour by the students. This kind of situation has to be handled with great sensitivity, but given firm direction the students can learn a great deal from the interchange. These are real life situations in a real context that deal, for many student teachers, with the theoretical issues formerly discussed only at university. Students attest to the amount they learn from them. Imagination and effort are called for on the part of the mentor teachers to use what they take so much for granted, the school environment, as a 'lecture room' for a teacher education session.

The Skills Needed for Effective Mentoring

The problem of how the task of the supervising teacher is now changed is one of the themes and tensions that run through the literature on mentoring. The primary function of schools is to provide learning opportunities for young people. When teachers are asked to take on the role of teacher educator, which is what is expected of them in the expanded role of mentor, they are being asked to resolve the tensions between the roles of classroom teacher and teacher educator.

Teachers as supervisors and mentors will continue to do what they have done so ably in the past. Indeed, it could be said that it is the success of what they have done under the guise of supervision that has caused the change in teacher education to take place. Students have found what they have learnt in schools so useful that they have asked for more of their course to be taught in the school. Teachers will continue to care for and nurture student teachers as they practice their skills. They will continue to pass on their tips for best practice. But now, teachers are being asked to do more than this. They are being asked to make the links between theory and practice that used to be made mainly at the university.

Mentoring, as opposed to supervision, requires a new set of skills and competencies for the teacher — skills and competencies that are different from those of supervision. Teachers now have to move from the nurturing, caring paradigm outlined in Chapter 3 to a more comprehensive and extended program. The result is that teacher supervisors have to be trained into this new role which is being variously named but is being most commonly called 'mentor'.

Teacher education staff at the University of Newcastle-on-Tyne in their *School Based Secondary PGCE Course Pilot Study Proposals for September 1992* address the problems that accompany the moving into schools of some of the theoretical material previously taught in Higher Education Institutions. In their document of information for schools they say:

2.4   Training should not be focused solely on the acquisition of classroom teaching skills, but should provide enhanced opportunities for students' full professional development across all aspects of school life including pastoral care, special needs, school organisation and management, cross-curricular issues and extra-curricular activities.

2.5   While much can be learned from observing good teachers in action in the classroom, the training programme should be based on a wider model of learning than 'apprentice-ship'. Students must be made to reflect critically upon their school based experiences, re-conceptualise their naive notions of teaching and incorporate research findings from beyond their school experience into their developing understanding of the teaching/learning process.

2.6   The school-based and university-based elements of the course should not be sharply divided but should inter-relate, complement and build upon each other. University tutors should contribute alongside teachers to the school-based components and teachers should participate in ses-sions at the university.

The document goes on to ask:

How much is there structured observation and the collection of data which will form the basis for critical reflection, analysis and discussion?

and to make the following suggestions to mentor teachers:

[There could be] A program of short, practical exercises, such as tracking a student throughout a day, or tracking a teacher. These should be linked to both curriculum and professional (general issues) studies components of the course.

School-based tutorials/seminars involving both school mentors and university tutors should provide a forum for the discussion and analysis of issues arising from the programme of structured observations and exercises. They should provide the opportunity to consider wider research findings and evidence from contexts other than the specific partnership school.

Immediately the difference is obvious between what supervising teachers were saying about their role in Chapter 3 and what the reflective paradigm exemplified above is asking of the role of mentoring. There are few studies that tell us about the character of what is now being called mentoring in the UK. Such lists as the above are helpful as a beginning to teasing out the new skills and competencies that have to be added to those of supervision.

Because so much of the teacher education program is now delegated to the school, including the teaching of subject method, teachers are expected to be abreast of the developments in their own areas of curriculum expertise and of education in general. For example, a teacher of English should have a bibliography of helpful books on the theory of the teaching of English — Language and Literature. They should also, in England and Wales, be familiar with the National Curriculum documents and the National Assessment documents as they apply to their subject area.

On the practical side, mentor teachers need to know how to manage an enquiry model of teaching and learning. By experiencing this, practice student teachers will be encouraged to reflect on their practice and ask for reasons before adopting behaviours and practices as their own. Teachers need to be open to the new ideas of the student teacher and allow a degree of risk-taking to occur, while setting limits. Mentors will also need the skill of examining critically their own practice and be open to change.

The model more familiar to student teachers is the behaviourist model in which a teacher tells a student the best way to behave in the classroom and expects imitation. There is necessarily an element of imitation in all student teacher/mentor teacher relationships. Imitation of exemplary practice is to be desired. But it is to be hoped that students will, under this changed system of school-based teacher education become more discriminating in their selection of behaviours to imitate as they become more reflective and analytical.

In a *post-practicum* survey carried out with primary teacher trainees at UNE in 1992 such comments as the following were common when students were asked what weakened their commitment to teaching during the *practicum*:

The way the teacher taught his class. I didn't agree with his way and felt the children were not benefiting from it.

I was expected to teach just what she had programmed for —
there wasn't much room for me to plan my own content.

My teacher seemed a little reluctant to let me get in and teach.
She was always saying, 'Why don't you do this . . .'

I do not want to end up like some of the teachers I saw on
practicum.

He butted in when I was teaching and sometimes started the
lesson for me.

He was very sexist and narrow-minded in that I didn't get to
explore many of my own techniques.

She provided lesson outlines that I had to comply with and
build my lessons around.

Not letting me do lessons my way.

The above students are discriminating between behaviours with
which they feel personally compatible and behaviours they want to
discard. The supervising teachers of these students appear to have been
in the functionalist, behaviourist mode, endeavouring to make the students conform to a standard practice. The worst fears of the critics of
school-based teacher education will be realised if that kind of supervision continues under the new system. Students will become clones
of their supervising teachers, and this need not necessarily be a good
thing. The students must be permitted to think for themselves, to
experiment (within safe limits), to rehearse their good ideas in a safe
environment where, to use computer user-friendly language, they are
permitted 'to recover gracefully from errors'.

Mentors need to be able to focus the student's attention on pupils'
learning styles and on the individual differences that have to be taken
into account in particular contexts. In Australia, this is becoming a more
pressing need as pupils with learning difficulties and special needs are
being integrated more and more into mainstream classes.

Because the task of mentor teachers is now more pivotal, they will
be expected to be highly motivated themselves and will be able to
expect the highest standards from the student teachers. This means that
they must be able to model the highest standards of professional behaviour themselves. In Australia the Advanced Skills Teacher (AST) is
being seen as the person in the school to take on the role of mentoring

the student teachers who come to the school. ASTs are appointed because of their skills in the profession and it is seen as part of their duties to pass on those skills to new teachers.

Mentors will also have to have skills of team leadership as there will be a team of subject tutors and others working with the student teachers. They will need to be efficient in their communication processes, so that materials and information are disseminated at the times when they are needed. They will need to have arbitration skills if problems develop between subject mentors and student teachers. And they will need to be able to liaise with the university tutors if there are real concerns. They will need to be able to keep accurate and useful records of the processes.

Mentors should have skills in both formative and summative evaluation techniques. Because they have the students with them for such a long period of time, they should give constant feedback, set targets for the next lesson and the next day and the next week, and have sessions of formative evaluation as the *practicum* progresses. In order to give meaningful feedback on lessons, mentor teachers need to be able to articulate curriculum principles and method processes and be observant and analytical. They need to be able to focus on what went well in a lesson, and what did not go well, and be able to analyse and to interrogate the processes in a helpful way that will lead to the professional development of the student teacher. They need to be able to set achievable targets for the student teacher in line with the student's performance each day.

The mentors need to be familiar with whole-school organisation so that they are able to advise and guide the student teacher through the 'political' maze of a busy school. In New South Wales in the last five years many changes have taken place in the structure of the Department of School Education. The self-managing school is a reality. Global budgeting in schools is affecting resourcing. Staffing and transfer regulations have changed. A National Curriculum is being constructed, and new syllabuses are being produced by the Board of Studies at regular intervals. The mentor teacher will need to be able to lead the student teacher through the maze of changes. The same is true of the situation in schools in England and Wales, with the National Curriculum and National Assessment. The student teachers, generally, need to be made familiar with the latest government documents on education.

This list of skills and competencies for the new role of mentor raises two questions. How does the busy teacher fit this extra work into an already overcrowded workload? And, what schemes need to be put into place to train teachers into the role of teacher educator? It is

surprising in the light of their busy-ness that many teachers are prepared willingly to take on the role of mentor.

Resourcing the Program

In the United Kingdom the resource implications of this increased contribution by schools to teacher education are being recognised. If a
student attracts about £4000 as a grant from the government for a PGCE
course, and two-thirds of that course is carried out in schools, logic
would seem to dictate that two-thirds of the money should be allocated
to schools. This would usually go towards additional staffing. School
teachers now have to carry out, efficiently, the extra program of teacher
education as well as taking part in the school's normal program and
main task of teaching children.

Departments and Schools of Education in universities are resist-
ing paying two-thirds of the money to schools, because the student
grant money is their 'life blood'. They are taxed about one-third of the
money by the central administration of the university, and if a further
two thirds went to schools, they would have no money to run their
departments.

If they suggested to the central university administration that the
'claw back' or 'top slicing' of one-third is excessive in the light of the
fact that the student teachers are not on campus using the general
facilities for two-thirds of the year, they are likely to be confronted with
the suggestion that the award is obviously not a university award and
should be handed over completely to the schools. In November 1992,
there was a strong rumour that the DfE might take over the award of
the PGCE. This would be disastrous for many Departments of Education in universities. They would have no money to fund their research.

The resourcing of the new scheme in England is fraught with difficulties. Each university is negotiating an agreement with schools for
the moment, and most universities are funding each student in a school
with from £500 to £1000. If the school has ten students in training at
one time, it could have £10,000 added to the school budget. As this
money does not go to the payment of teachers for supervision and
mentoring as it does in Australia, the school in England is free to use
the money as the school needs dictate.

If the same scheme were to be adopted in Australia, the problems
would be even more difficult to overcome. For about twenty years,
supervising teachers have been paid a sum of about $21.00 per day. For
this reason, the number of days of *practicum* have been reduced to a

minimum. The equivalent course to the PGCE has about 40 days of *practicum*, compared with 120 days in England. Until the *nexus* between payment and supervision is broken, it is not feasible to lengthen the *practicum* in Australia. At the time of writing, the case against the National Practice Teaching Award is being heard in the Arbitration Commission. The results of these deliberations will not be known until 1994. The Award is being opposed by the Commonwealth Government amongst others. It is obvious that they realise that any plans to make teacher education more school-based, are contingent on the Award being repealed. The Commonwealth Government has plans for a National Professional Development Fund, into which would be put the moneys now set aside for practice teaching. This Fund would be accessed by any teachers who wanted to take part in a Professional Development Project. At discussions with unions, universities and employing authorities, this suggestion of a Professional Development Fund has been firmly rejected by the unions and the universities — the unions because they can see that their members are going to be doing supervision without payment, and the universities because they can see themselves being denied access to the half to one million dollars (depending on numbers of students) that they receive in their budgets each year to pay teachers for *practicum* supervision. There is also a concern that if the universities are not seen to be employing the supervising teachers, albeit casually, they will lose some ownership of the award.

Conclusion

In this chapter the change of the teacher's role from supervisor to mentor has been examined. Some general suggestions have been made for ways in which a curriculum of practice teaching can be put in place in schools that are working in partnership with universities in initial teacher education courses.

The next four chapters outline the ways in which four specific partnerships are working in new school-based or school-focused initial teacher education programs.

Chapter 5

Towards Empowerment: An Approach to School-Based Mentoring

David Reid

The Manchester Context

The importance of context in educational change is paramount. Curriculum development, pedagogical reform, philosophical stance and continual professional development are just a few examples of those issues which are susceptible to the contextual circumstances within which an educational establishment, be it school or university, has to work on a day-to-day basis. Context has a disproportionate influence on the effectiveness of reform. Even schools within a few hundred yards from each other can legitimately hold radically different views on many issues, views which will be reflected in the structures and the processes which they will use to fulfil their perceived roles.

The University of Manchester has been training teachers for over a century. It works with schools over the 750 square miles of the conurbation of Greater Manchester, many of whose staff received their initial training or who have obtained higher diplomas and degrees at the University. The secondary Post Graduate Certificate of Education (PGCE) course is of medium size, training some 180 students annually. Due to historical accident it is a course which is strong in the 'shortage subjects', all of which attract government bursaries to encourage students into the teaching profession (Biology, Chemistry, Physics, Mathematics, Technology, French, German and Spanish). English and Economics are also represented as main subjects. However, the course is weak in the traditional humanities subjects such as Geography, History, Religious Education and Drama, which are offered only at subsidiary level. Up to half of our postgraduate entry comes directly from first degree courses, but a substantial proportion typically has experience, for example, in industry or the professions, from working abroad, as parents, or as research students. Thus many students bring to the course a wealth of experience gleaned from outside the education profession. This not only gives them a confidence and maturity in taking responsibility for their own learning, but it has a positive influence on the attitudes of their less experienced peers. It also means that the student body is experientially heterogeneous, a phenomenon which has encouraged individualisation on a course where time is always at a premium.

Traditionally our students have had access to a rich variety of schools and cultural ecologies during their training year. From the more deprived inner city areas of Moss Side to the leafy suburbs of middle-class Hale and Bowdon, the philosophies, aims and structures of the schools vary greatly. Comprehensive 11–16, 11–18, coeducational and single sex schools; grammar and secondary modern schools; voluntary aided religious foundation schools (mainly Roman Catholic, Anglican and Jewish); grant maintained schools; independent schools; sixth form, tertiary and metropolitan colleges and special education schools have all made major contributions to the provision of school practice over the years.

University tutors largely welcomed the government's proposal that all student teachers spend a minimum of 120 days of their 180 day PGCE course physically in the schools. This represents a 66 per cent school-based course, which for Manchester would be an increase of some 10 per cent. Our experience with an earlier government innovation (the Articled Teachers scheme) had shown that an 80 per cent school-based experience has not allowed the student teachers sufficient time for reflectivity.

In 1991 a report by Her Majesty's Inspectorate (HMI) had been generally sympathetic to the principle of an increase in the school-based element of one-year PGCE secondary courses, although it was careful to point out that such an increase would not be the panacea for teacher training that the political far right sometimes appeared to suppose. HMI made a number of caveats which can be summarised as concerns about issues of quality control and communication between the various partners. The government introduced its criteria and procedures for the new course in *Circular 9/92*, which, in addition to requiring all secondary PGCE courses to be 66 per cent school-based by September 1994, also introduced a set of minimal competences against which the government's quality control body (The Council for the Accreditation of Teacher Education, CATE) would accredit courses. In addition, universities had to demonstrate that the schools had been equal partners with the HEIs in the planning and management of the courses. They also required that student teachers should have experience in more than one secondary school.

David Reid

A Theoretical Stance

The tensions which currently exist in secondary schools in England and Wales were not going to be eased by the imposition of yet another educational innovation which would alter the role of the schools, increase the workload of their staff, and, if past experiences were anything to go by, be under-resourced. One major unanswered question was how the schools would (or could) respond to a role which would involve them more in the permeation of theory and practice, in the sharing of ideas and philosophies, in encouraging creative reflectivity and in the exploration generally of educational ideas that went far beyond their traditional role of instilling technical classroom skills.

It is one of the strengths of the English secondary school that it has been able to respond so positively to massive change over the last five years or so, in terms of, for example, the introduction of the General Certificate of Secondary Education and the National Curriculum. Other countries, equally as well resourced, have not shown such resilience. Stake and Easely, for example (1978), have demonstrated the recidivist nature of the 1960s curriculum reform movement in the US. Despite massive financial backing, the excellence of the new curricula themselves, and the vigour with which the teachers prepared themselves for the innovations, by the mid-1970s there was little evidence of change in the classroom. Such intransigence has resulted in the science and mathematics achievements of American children in the 1980s being amongst the lowest in the world (Lapointe, Mead and Phillips 1989).

One of the most obvious features of the British secondary school is its hierarchical departmental structure (Brown and Reid 1990). To those of us brought up in the system it is such an obvious feature that it is often overlooked. Yet it performs a number of important functions, not the least of which is the way the classroom teachers within a department are nurtured, supported and encouraged to share their problems, and take responsibility for a creative pedagogy (Reid 1993). It is the departmental structure that empowers teachers within a collegial support system and enables a more permanent response to innovation than is seen in countries where teachers have to rely more upon their own resources. Not only does the departmental structure encourage and support individual responsibility, it also releases middle and senior management from concerns of everyday classroom events to concentrate on wider issues, such as the implementation of local management of schools, devolved budgets, and even grant maintained status. Generally, empowerment makes schools more effective and rewarding places for both teachers and children. Taken all in all, Hargreaves and Hopkins (1991) argue that the empowered school is the school which responds to the challenges of change by recreating its own vision, by redefining management to support change and by releasing the energy and confidence to put its ideas into practice.

Empowering the department-based mentor means the recognition by all concerned that it is the cheek-by-jowl nature of the student teacher/mentor relationship that should be allowed to determine when, and to as large an extent as possible, what school-based experiences the student teacher is exposed to. It is a model of mentoring which argues that the final responsibility for the professional development of the student teacher resides jointly with the student teacher and his or her mentor, and not with the University tutor or any senior member of the school staff. It becomes the job of HEI to monitor that role, but not to interfere with the way in which those responsibilities are carried through.

Problems Inherent in Mentor Empowerment

While accepting, *a priori*, the principle of mentor empowerment, it now behoves the University to analyse the kinds of problems that such a unique approach to mentoring might attract. In summary the list can look somewhat daunting.

- There is no guarantee that the departmental structure of the school will support mentor empowerment in the same way that I have claimed it supports curricular innovation. Mentor empowerment is a form of continuing professional development, which is a more personal thing than curriculum innovation, and of which 'the news about meaningful change is often discouraging' (Dlin and Levi 1993).
- The roles of mentor, student teacher, tutor and senior co-ordinating teacher within the school will not always be perceived as complementary. The empowered mentor will be challenged at times by the legitimate perceptions of the other three main players, who may even differ amongst themselves. The empowered mentor has to expect to cope with the ambiguities that will arise between concerned adults.
- Empowered mentors are positively encouraged, during their training, to work unashamedly to the very strengths of provision and variation in philosophical approach for which they

were selected in the first instance. These will, of course, vary widely across the range of training establishments. This appears to contrast markedly with the spirit of uniformity of experience required by CATE, which explicitly requires that: 'HEI and all schools in partnership with them will need to collaborate in ensuring that student teachers undertake similar tasks and gain similar experience, wherever their time in school is spent.'

Mentor empowerment encourages an individualised approach, and depends upon the professional interpretation of the mentor's response to problems. No one mentor can be expected to provide a 'comprehensive' course of professional training.

- All student teachers at Manchester receive training in at least four schools. A preliminary practice in a primary school (10 days); their partner school (70 days); a second secondary school (30 days); and a specialist, often special educational needs school (10 days). It is essential that each school is aware of the experiences which a student teacher has accrued and the specific role which it is expected to play. Communication in such a multi-based provision will be of paramount importance, as HMI were quick to recognise in their 1991 Report.
- Externally imposed quality control mechanisms are a threat to mentor empowerment. They limit the responsibility a mentor can take in making relationships with their partner student and in doing so undermine the whole concept of professional empowerment. Yet quality assurance is probably the major factor by which the university course will be accredited by CATE (McSharry and Reid 1993).
- PGCE course planning becomes a major responsibility of the empowered mentor. It is essential that the teachers being trained for mentorship agree about the roles of the various players and plan the course accordingly. The temptation the tutors have to resist at all costs is to succumb to teacher pressure to 'tell us how to do it'. Slowly, and often at the risk of anarchy in the training sessions, the mentors must come to realise that, in the empowerment business, 'the process is the product'.

The crucial change in attitude of mentors to teacher training had to be from involvement (as it always had been) to commitment. General 'Stormin' Norman Schwartzkopf is reputed to have told his troops, on the eve of the Gulf War in 1991, that he required of them '100 per cent commitment'. The difference between involvement and commitment is a bit like the great American breakfast of ham and eggs. The chicken is involved, the pig is committed. For a teacher, commitment comes from taking joint responsibility for the development of another professional at every stage of the learning process, from course planning to induction. It does not come from prescriptions imposed by others.

From Involvement to Commitment

The dilemma faced was essentially one of quality control, and how this might best be secured across a multiplicity of providers each of whom would be constantly encouraged during the training process to work to those idiosyncratic strengths and convictions which characterise their professional lives. It was the characteristics of the individual classroom teachers in which we were most interested, and not the school (and, for example, its position in the league table) or the interests of senior management (who also had their own hidden agenda — for example, the opportunities which the scheme provided for free staff development, the income that student teachers would generate, and the *kudos* that would attach to their school as a training institution). In essence we wanted to select teachers who:

- expressed a desire to work with adults in teacher education and who were aware of the differences between teaching children and adults;

- were proven good practitioners;

- were independent thinkers holding a spectrum of different though legitimate convictions about the teaching of children and ITE. The dilemma is summarised in Figure 1 below.

Clearly, it is 'A' in the model which is the key to converting mentor attitude from a traditional involvement in training to a commitment to teacher education. But by giving the mentors the kind of responsibility which will ensure commitment on their terms, the very outcome which will guarantee accreditation by CATE (see 'B' in Figure 1) is challenged. We shall deal first with the absolute necessity to ensure that the course fulfils the requirements of CATE, for without accreditation by the Secretary of State we should have no course.

Figure 1: *Ensuring commonality of output while encouraging variety of input*

The Position
ITE through empowerment

The Problem
solving the dilemma among:

A	B
Role of mentor and input control	*Role of student and output control*
encouraging variety and independence	ensuring commonality of student
of mentor input and responsibility	experience and responsibility

C
Role of University and Process Control
Mechanisms of output control:
the RoAD document

Above all else a PGCE course of ITE should stand or fall on the basis of its product. There is a powerful argument put by government that it is the competences of the students upon completion of the course that should be the final arbiter for course accreditation.

The DfE, in *Circular 9/92*, outline five minimal holistic competences against which student teachers shall be adjudged to have passed or failed the course, and each one of them subsumes another half dozen or so sub-competences. These minimal competences are competence in:

- subject knowledge;
- subject application;
- classroom management;
- the assessment and recording of pupils' progress;
- realising the need for future professional development.

Manchester, in common with many other universities, has produced a Record of Achievement and Development (RoAD) based on the minimal competences prescribed by the DfE. As far as the student teachers are concerned, this is the single most important document they meet on the course. In addition to the minimal competences, the RoAD contains competences agreed by mentors during training. These vary from subject to subject. Thus, the holistic competence 'subject knowledge' has many more sub-competences attached to it in Technology than in any other subject area since technology graduates usually specialise in one particular subject area — say design technology —

and will have little expertise in home economics, electronics, information technology and so on. The technology mentors also decided that their RoAD should require all technologists-in-training to pass a first aid examination.

Mentors discussed the RoAD not only with the University tutors, but also with student teachers currently on the course and using a RoAD prototype. Advice from the mentors on RoAD format was sought in five areas:

- in defining holistic competences in their subject area in addition to the minimal competences laid down by the DfE;
- in defining sets of sub-competences for all of the holistic competences, both minimal and additional;
- in defining specific criteria which prescribed a sub-competence;
- in defining specific criteria which described a sub-competence;
- in producing a number of action statements which evidenced a sub-competence.

The science mentors felt that an ability to communicate in science lessons deserved an additional holistic competence. The sub-competences they attached to Communicating in Science were:

- ability to develop a social climate which encourages a work-oriented atmosphere;
- ability to use appropriate questioning techniques;
- ability to obtain and use feedback from pupil talk;
- ability to write materials appropriate to the learning skills of different pupils;
- ability to use appropriate language, including technical language, when talking to children;
- awareness of the importance of non-verbal behaviours in the classroom.

Prescriptive criteria were seldom produced. Failure to achieve such a criterion would result in automatic failure of the entire course. One obvious example would be failure by a student teacher to satisfy a criterion which prescribed the safe use of potentially dangerous equipment or materials.

Mentors found it relatively easy to agree on both the descriptive criteria, by which a level of competence can be agreed, and examples of student teacher behaviour which would act as evidence that a descriptive criterion had been satisfied.

Figure 2: A Page from RoAD

Class Management
(to create and maintain a purposeful and orderly environment for the pupils)

prescriptive criterion: noise levels controlled

descriptive criteria: tidy classroom
                      organised resources
                      respected code of behaviour
                      no eating or drinking
                      no bags on the floor

evidence: children are lined up quietly outside the classroom before they are allowed entry;
student displays children's work on the walls;
children raise hands if they want to answer a question — no shouting normally allowed.

Student notes:
(On the rest of the page the student makes notes on other kinds of action statements that might provide evidence of competence; where in the course s/he might expect to obtain provision in any special skills required to obtain and then demonstrate competence (including library books, or videos in the resource centre, newspaper articles another student might have seen, etc.); any targets that s/he might begin setting her/himself in terms of long term competence (for example in developing computer skills) and any accredited prior learning that might be admissible. Such information is discussed with tutor and/or mentor in conference sessions.)

Figure 2 represents the first of two pages allocated to a sub-competency — in this example the sub-competency is Classroom Management. The first half of the second page is formatted for targets that the student teachers can be set or can set themselves, and the time scale for achieving them. The remaining half page lists the students' achievements in the sub-competence, together with the dates and evidence of achievement. These can include skills brought to the course as accredited prior learning. For example, an English student who worked as a secretary will have word processing skills.

Using RoAD

Resonant throughout this chapter is the radically new role which the student teachers will assume in the school-based course. Remember that we are not dealing with young 18-year-olds fresh from school, but with mature learners every one of whom possesses a first degree and up to half of whom will be considerably more experienced than this. In the first few days of the course a great deal of stress will be put on ensuring that student teachers are thoroughly conversant with the content of RoAD and its function. Skills of target setting will be practised, and cases of accredited prior learning evidenced, agreed and recorded. The students' role as instigators of conferencing and recorders of achievement will be explained. Without apposite evidence, end-of-year references will be weak and applications for posts jeopardised.

However, students can only make relevant choices and demands when they are aware of the provision to which they are entitled and the sources from which it can be expected. It is at this point that we turn to 'A' in our model in Figure 1, having satisfied ourselves that, in principle, commonality of output is feasible if the RoAD instrument is properly utilised.

Input Control: The Training Curriculum

Mentors were required to complete a Training Curriculum, in which they were to lay out in detail the school-based training they intended to provide their student teachers. This requirement serves a number of purposes:

- it focuses mentors' attention onto relevant areas during discussion in training;
- it provides a detailed outline of each mentor's provision, so that student teachers have a basis for their selection of a partner school and tutors can be informed of the extent to which the mentor is fulfilling his or her side of the bargain;
- it allows the university to validate each mentor's provision, thus increasing quality control;
- it is a constant reminder to the mentor of what they should be doing at any time of the year.

Each Training Curriculum was to consist of four elements.

1 A *curriculum vitae*

This element is again part of course input quality control. The University, and ultimately the accreditation body, has a responsibility to assure itself that each mentor possesses the basic qualifications for the job. Evidence of appropriate degree, satisfactory experience working with children and adults, and an active record of continuing professional development was sought. The *curriculum vitae* is extracted from the Training Curriculum and filed confidentially in the Director's office. Student teachers do not have access to this information.

2 A personal statement

Because of the wide diversity of mentor background, it is important that student teachers have some information on the educational pedigree of the person with whom they will be working closely. Mentors are asked to write a page or so about their experiences as a teacher, and their broad philosophy of the educational process.

3 The basis for partnership

The third component of the Training Curriculum is an extended document called 'The basis for partnership at . . . school'. In this section the mentors are invited to describe the unique features of their school as a training establishment. Many mentors include professional publications of the sort used to inform prospective parents about the school, and containing examples of the best work of the children. This section of the Training Curriculum anticipates a more recent DfE publication called the 'Parents' Charter' (DfE 1993b), which requires schools to publish details of school life which are likely to help parents in the selection of a school for their children.

4 The Training Curriculum

The curriculum itself details the week-by-week provision that the school will make to the training of students. It is based upon a number of criteria devised by the University tutors in discussion with mentors, and against which each curriculum is validated:

a a statement of the mentor's role;
b evidence of progression of student experience throughout the year;
c evidence of coherence of provision between the school and University;
d evidence of the unique contribution to be made by the school;
e evidence of the variety of experiences to be provided;
f a statement of procedures for conferencing;
g a statement on competences;
h details of assessment procedures.

The Training Curriculum is crucial to mentor empowerment and quality control. During validation the University tutors could, and often did, require mentors to be more explicit when it was felt that the students would need more information to fulfil their own role in the program.

Detail of the Training Curriculum

The Role of the Mentor

While it was possible to prescribe a list of complimentary roles of mentor, tutor and student teacher, the spirit of the exercise is to encourage the mentors to define their own roles within general guidelines. In some schools we knew that the senior co-ordinating teachers were in the habit of meeting all the student teachers for an hour or so each week to discuss wider educational issues such as interviewing techniques, and the role of parents in school life. In other schools this was left to the subject mentors. Three independent study packs were written by the University to support mentors and student teachers; Special Educational Needs, Multicultural Education, and The Whole School Curriculum. The schools are expected to support the student teachers in the completion of the school-based exercises in the packs by facilitating introductions to specialist staff and arranging for the students to meet and talk to relevant classes and individual children.

Evidence of Progression

It was a requirement of the Training Curriculum that it evidenced opportunities for both qualitative and quantitative progression of student teacher experiences through the year. This was perceived as the vertical dimension of the Curriculum (see Figure 3). Implicit evidence of qualitative progression was acceptable, and it is recognised that progression is not always a linear process. Management skills developed to deal with small groups, for example, are often inappropriate for large groups. Quantitative progression was looked for in the amount of exposure to a particular experience, and it was agreed that the mentors must use their professional expertise in deciding the amount of whole class teaching a particular student teacher should experience at any particular time. Some students would never cope with more than a 50 per cent timetable, others might be ready for a 50 per cent timetable by Christmas in the UK, and an 80 per cent timetable by the summer.

Figure 3: Progression — the vertical dimension of the curriculum

---

Progression in classroom experiences

   Beginning of Partnership

      Observation;
      Working with individual children;
      Working with small groups;
      Team teaching;
      Whole class teaching, limited timetable;
      Shadowing technician/ child/ teacher;
      Attention to questioning techniques — from simple closed questions to
         more sophisticated open questions;
      Attention to assessment skills;
      Pastoral interests in individuals;
      Simple management skills — management of whole classes;
      Whole class teaching, 50 per cent timetable;
      Curriculum development skills;
      Whole class teaching, to 80 per cent timetable;
      . . . and so on

   End of partnership

Evidence of coherence

The second dimension to the Curriculum was perceived as horizontal. While the ITE course would focus on classroom experiences in the first instance (Figure 3), it was clear that these would have to be supported by departmental, school and community experiences on the one hand, and University provision on the other. The question as to how provision from these different sources could be co-ordinated was important. Many HMI reports in recent years have commented adversely on the permeation of school and university provision in ITE — often in simplistic terms of the permeation of 'practice and theory'.

Criticisms by the far right in teacher education (for example, Lawler 1990 and 1993, and O'Heare 1993) argue vociferously that the place to train teachers is in the classroom, and not in HEI, where:

> As anyone [sic] who has been on these courses will tell you, on all but the best of them there is a grindingly anti-competitive ethos. Pupil failure and bad behaviour are regarded as symptoms of social and personal deprivation rather than faults needing correction. There is an endless mouthing of the mantras of anti-sexism and anti-racism. (O'Heare 1993)

Aware that such criticisms, while wildly exaggerated, nevertheless raise an important philosophical issue, the University made the decision to be explicit in demonstrating that ITE at Manchester would be seen to have as its driving source the students' classroom and school experiences. Necessary theoretical underpinnings of and reflections about issues would be consequent upon such experiences. Hence, the mentors are required to concentrate on classroom experiences in the first instance and only then to consider appropriate coherence with provision from other sources.

To illustrate the concept of *coherence* we can take three imaginary instances occurring at progressively later stages through the year. An example of an experience that student teachers are likely to encounter earlier rather than later in the year is the need to write a worksheet for a group or a whole class of children. The mentor, at a conferencing session, will discuss the departmental policy on worksheet production, indicate stocks available, in-house styles of writing and reprographic facilities. At the same time, the University tutor will inform on the theory of worksheet production, how readability is influenced by such things as conceptual content, style of writing, complexity of syntax, format and layout, use of pictorial devices and so on. It is, of course quite impossible for the University to be able to respond on an *ad hominem* basis in every case. Subject tutors, therefore, in discussion with mentors, agreed a broad timetable of inputs of this kind, supported by a core lecture program. These are published in the Secondary Course Handbook, and in each subject handbook. This permits some flexibility as to when a student teacher starts to write worksheets. However, to increase this flexibility many subject tutors have written subject-based independent study packs so that when coherence of timing collapses, coherence of content can be retained. A good example of this is provided by the Centre for Science and Technology Education, whose staff have been working for the past three years, in conjunction with the DfE, on the production of a comprehensive series of such packages. These have been piloted in schools around the country and have proved so successful that they are to be published in early 1994 by HMSO (Reid, Ryles and McSharry 1994a,b,c,d,e,f,g and h). There is likely to be a proliferation of such packages in the near future. HMSO are also publishing parallel packs in English and Mathematics, together with a series of core units common to all subjects. The Open University is also preparing materials.

An example of a *school experience* more likely to occur during the middle part of an ITE course is a parents' evening. One of the competences required of newly qualified teachers is an ability to communicate with parents. The University core lecture program and associated workshops sessions deal with the role of parents in the second term.

A late experience might involve the wider community. Here the student teacher might be required to visit school students on industrial experience, liaise with local industry, or appraise a child's experience of their industrial link. Student teachers may be given the task of forging better links with feeder schools or with the post-16 establishments to which the children will be transferring at the end of Year 12. This element is built into the final term's work at the University.

The unique contribution of the partner school

Schools and teachers were selected for partnership on the basis that they were centres of excellence that could make a major contribution to ITE. Examples of excellence in certain schools are their work with:

- intellectually gifted children;
- post-16 students;
- children whose first language is not English;
- industry;
- children in inner city areas;
- girls;
- children from ethnic minorities;
- children gifted in sport or music;
- children who are boarders in the school;
- children with learning difficulties;
- religious foundations;
- foreign countries, etc.

A variety of experience

The new form of training gave mentors an opportunity to break free of the traditional form of 'block teaching practice' in which student teachers were placed in front of as many classes as possible for as long as possible. Student teachers would be in their partner school throughout the year, both on intermittent (two or three days a week) and on extended periods of continuous school practice. Mentors were required to be creative in the use of their student's time in school, and to use them as a human resource to the advantage of the pupils in diverse professional ways. They could be given limited pastoral responsibilities, functions within the subject department (contributing to INSET, organising departmental meetings, writing to parents, leading small working parties in areas in which they had specialist skills, setting examinations, liaising with other departments and so on), developing computing and information technology elements of curriculum, and community links.

Procedures for conferencing

Since conferencing will play a vital part in empowering student teachers to take responsibility for ensuring their own professional development, it was essential that the University was satisfied of the procedures the mentor intended to put into place. There was unease amongst many mentors that they might have insufficient time to do this adequately, as only a relatively small minority had managed to negotiate timetabled release for the purpose. In the event the University was forced to accept a statement of professional intent of the sort 'appropriate time will be made available for conferencing'. This will require careful monitoring.

Competences

Not all schools will address all the competences. This does not matter provided that there is a clear statement as to which ones will not be addressed, so that student teachers can search them out elsewhere. Not all schools had sufficient Information Technology (IT) capability to satisfy the competences for example. Judicious selection of second school practice would form part of the remedial process.

Assessment

Mentors were required to be explicit about how they would set targets in RoAD, when they would write formative and summative reports on student teachers, and how his information would be related to tutors and student teachers.

Discussion

In spite of all the efforts put into maximising course communication and quality control we are only too well aware that there remain a number of imponderables which could have major and adverse impact on the efficacy of the course; no doubt this is a feature of all reform.

We know that we have done our best, and we believe our best to be good enough. Nevertheless, it is worth rehearsing some features of a mentor empowerment model of ITE that should lead to misgivings amongst the readers of this chapter.

Are we, for example, shifting too much of the burden of responsibility for their professional development upon the student teachers themselves? Empowering students, like empowering mentors, is a risky business. It is designed to ensure that individual students will struggle, especially in the early stages of the course, with a new kind of learning. This is an inescapable element of the empowerment process, where 'the process is the product'. And do the mentors appreciate the struggle the students face? And if they do (for they have experienced it now for themselves), have they the resources at their disposal appropriately to nourish, support and challenge (in that order) the students? All this has been discussed with the mentors, but have they internalised their new role? Are they, at the beginning of a new school year, so child-oriented once again that they make too many assumptions about adult learning?

Have we gone too far in encouraging the unique and individualised nature of the empowered mentor's function? McIntyre and Hagger (1993) warn of the dangers of 'arbitrariness and idiosyncrasy' inherent in mentoring at the best of times. We believe that our collective quality assurance procedures (Williams and Loder 1990) are adequate insurance against this, but we are still supremely (and rightly so) dependent upon the professional integrity of individuals.

The training program discussed in this chapter might have the appearance of being a logically thought-out exercise. To some extent, of course, it was. The mentors attended for 8 two-and-a-half hour twilight sessions, for which they were each paid a total of £400 plus minimal expenses and were provided with a buffet meal. They came with the expectation of being 'trained' as mentors, even though they had joined the program knowing that it was to be based on the principle of empowerment. Senior school management and school heads and principals were also aware of the philosophy underpinning the exercise — indeed it is true to say that many of them had elected to work with The University of Manchester for this very reason. It turned out that neither senior management, nor subject mentors, nor some tutors were fully prepared for the consequences! Senior management began to feel nervous that their traditional responsibilities were being transferred to sometimes relatively junior members of staff, and that they were not being kept sufficiently informed as to what their school was committing itself. In retrospect this was a failing on the part of the University, which we did our best to rectify once the seriousness of the situation had been made clear to us. It transpired, not that senior management were unwilling to release such responsibilities, but that, quite rightly, they had a 'need to know' what was transpiring. The biggest struggle was for the mentors themselves, who initially wanted to be told what their new responsibilities were to be. Some tutors found this difficult to handle, as discussion turned to argument and argument turned to frustration at the seeming impotence of the University to say clearly what was required. All this is part of the unnerving process of empowerment. For the most part, staff were able to resist informing in the way that the teachers initially required. Breakthroughs came at different times with different groups, and when they did, the learning curve started steeply and climbed rapidly, as the confidence instilled by the continued assurance that the teachers already knew the answers to the questions they were asking took effect. The result is that the course is genuinely a teacher-led course, and there is a real sense in which it can be said that each mentor 'owns' his or her contribution (the Training Curriculum). Among other things, this has made the 'agreement' which the DfE requires the universities to make with their partner schools, a very simple event. Unlike other universities, where pages of documentation are being produced which define the roles of the various partners, our agreement is a simple statement of professional intent, that a school 'intends to deliver the Training Curriculum written by the subject mentor and validated by the University'.

And what of continuing mentor development? We perceive mentoring 'in terms of the character of the relationship and the function it serves' (Daresh and Playko 1993) in contrast to the assumption that it can be defined by reference to formal roles. Like Daresh and Playko we believe that effective mentors need to model the principles of continuous learning and reflection that they are trying to instil into others. To this end our mentor training was designed in two stages. A first stage resulting in the production of individualised, validated Training Curricula, and a second stage in which the mentors are monitored as they put their curricula into effect during the first year of the new course. Each stage earns accredited prior learning for an MEd module, but only upon successful completion of Stage 2 do mentors receive their Certificate of Mentoring. A termly publication, 'Quality in Initial Teacher Education' (QUITE) is sent to all mentors, in which current teacher education issues are discussed and to which mentors are invited to contribute. Optimistic views for the future involve more tutor-teacher exchanges with the schools, and the evolution of action research by tutors and teachers in the schools as the full potential of partnership is realised.

Chapter 6

Towards More School-Based Initial Teacher Education

Chris Kellett

In the last two years, schools and Higher Education Institutions have been faced with considerable political pressure to ensure that initial teacher education becomes increasingly school-based. The original proposals from the Department for Education stated that 80 per cent of the Postgraduate Certificate in Education courses (PGCE) of 36 weeks should take place in schools. This figure was later reduced to a period of 24 weeks minimum, 66 per cent (DfE 1992). Even with this reduction to the time to be spent in schools, teachers who had worked alongside universities and colleges for some time providing supervision for students shared several concerns about their new roles and the increased responsibilities required by these changes. Time for the planning of the new courses was limited, the level of resourcing for the school element of the course in some instances was unknown at the outset, and in-service training for mentor teachers was minimal to begin with. Our previous work with student teachers as supervisor teachers had prepared us in part for the task that lay ahead, but new skills were required if we were to be able to liaise with colleagues in universities and colleges to plan courses. We had to be able to encourage and support colleagues in school to adapt to their roles as subject mentors and become contributors to the whole training program. In addition, we would have to work alongside student teachers to develop their understanding of the broader professional role of teachers, allowing reflection and questioning which would support the development of their knowledge and practice.

The new ITE involves considerable change for the mentor teachers and their colleagues in schools. Mentor teachers had previously been effective supervisors, helping students to plan, prepare and review lessons. Practical help was also given to allow students to settle into the life of a particular school effectively. But now the active co-operation and support of university staff, the school staff, and mentor teachers in other partner schools were essential to enable all those involved to feel confident in their ability to meet the training needs of student teachers when in schools. Details of how one school faced this extensive change in function, what the school training program entailed, reflections on these experiences and comment on the developing role of the mentor teacher are included in this chapter.

Early Links with the University

Fulford School is an 11–18 comprehensive school with 1000 pupils and is situated less than half a mile from the University of York. Over the years, strong links have been established between school departments and corresponding departments within the University. Members of Fulford staff and staff from other schools have been involved with the delivery of aspects of the PGCE curriculum courses and some option courses. Tutors in the University Department of Educational Studies have felt that the involvement of practising teachers has given student teachers contact with immediate, relevant and practical experience of the teaching role. Exposure to 'real' teachers has for some time been seen as an essential part of the professional development of students. These contacts became the roots of the partnership scheme established in 1992 between local schools and the University. It has almost become a tradition, particularly in languages, science and English curriculum areas, that Fulford has been one of the first ports of call for the University for the in-school support of student teachers. Importantly, the wider staff group, parents and pupils accept the presence of significant numbers of student teachers within classrooms. Their contributions to the life of the school have been, and are, valued although the responsibilities of supporting students in the development of their practice can be rather onerous at times. The general feeling amongst department colleagues tends to be that helping to train students is a role that they want very much to fulfil. This is especially so, since the student teacher has commitment, energy, new ideas, new skills, fresh and imaginative materials and, above all, enthusiasm to offer to the departments within which they work. It should be noted at this point that only four departments play a full role in supporting students, but colleagues from every other department have played their part by allowing student teachers to observe them working in the classroom. Moreover, other staff have also responded positively to requests from the students to allow them to participate in the classroom process.

Planning

Although early soundings of staff opinion indicated there was clearly positive support for the school's involvement with initial teacher education, many staff were concerned about the further demands which might face them when coping with the changes not only in their role, but also with the significant increase in school-based training. University staff shared these concerns and readily responded to requests for discussions and information. However, we also felt that it was essential to sort out our own thinking and plan for our involvement in the partnership scheme for 1992–93. We began by setting up a working party of staff in the Autumn term, 1991, to focus on issues of common concern and planning. All heads of the departments that were to be involved, other interested individuals, the school ITE co-ordinator and the deputy head in charge of initial teacher education formed the working party, eight staff in all.

Many concerns were expressed by members of the working party. Staff wanted to know:

- Would the pressure on staff be too great, as student training would be in addition to an already increased workload?
- What level of support would be available from the University tutors for school staff and student teachers?
- What strategies could be used to ensure a consistency of standard and approach between the University and the school?
- What numbers of students would we be asked to take?
- Would it be possible for us to participate in the selection and final assessment of students, as they would be spending the greater part of their training time in school?
- What would be the content of the Whole School Issues program and how would we staff the whole school sessions?
- What costs to the school would be incurred by our participation, i.e., staffing, and the effects of students' increased presence in the classroom on pupils?
- How would staff facilities cope with increased demand for their use?
- How much money would be transferred from the University to cover the costs of the provision of the program?

How We Answered These Concerns

It was essential for the working party to carry staff with them if ITE in school were to be successful. In this regard, the concern about pressure on staff was crucial. Everyone involved — staff, pupils and student teachers — would all suffer if we could not find a strategy which would help to lessen the pressure of the school's rapidly developing and increasing role in training. The appointment of an initial teacher education training co-ordinator was made and, in addition, the roles and responsibilities of members of staff were clearly defined. Curriculum area staff were then able to see that the co-ordinator would be undertaking many of the tasks which were causing concern for them, for example, expanding the reporting procedure to the University, and working more closely with University tutors. Included below are the details of the policy statement and role descriptions which are available to staff.

Initial Teacher Training Policy

It is the policy of Fulford School to work alongside Institutions of Higher Education in the delivery of initial teacher education. Senior management and school staff will offer appropriate programs of learning and teaching for student teachers.

Curriculum programs will be delivered by departmental staff. The Whole School Issues course and lunchtime seminars will be provided by the ITE co-ordinator. The content of these programs will be based on the requirements of the CATE statements of competence, i.e., subject knowledge, subject application, class management, assessment and recording of pupil progress and skills for further professional development.

The co-ordinator will work with colleagues in departments to provide an effective induction program and subsequently to organise the regular monitoring, evaluation and support of student progress. Student teachers will be encouraged to realise that their role is not simply confined to their curriculum area. They will be helped to understand the role of the form tutor and whole school issues and they will be required from the outset to participate actively in the life of the school as a whole.

Role of the ITE Co-ordinator

The co-ordinator is responsible for:

- working with the deputy responsible for ITE and servicing the ITE sub-committee;
- running student induction sessions and providing information pack on Fulford School;
- managing the school-based Whole School Issues program, i.e., organisation of the sessions and liaison with the individuals/departments involved;
- liaison with University tutors to develop Whole School Issues sessions appropriately;
- liaison with other institutions requiring student placements;
- negotiation with staff to enable students to be involved in tutor time, extra-curricular activities, duties, and school residential visits;
- provision of materials for all the above sessions;
- classroom observation — in particular, form tutor time and extra-curricular activities;
- providing and managing a support program for students;
- monitoring student progress in the identified areas of activity;
- reviewing discussions of students' progress with departments, University tutors and the students themselves;
- written assessment of students' classroom performance;
- liaising with University curriculum area tutors;
- providing formative and summative reports to the University on student progress;
- attendance at training meetings at the University;
- representing the interests of Fulford School in all meetings, for example, examiners meetings;
- record keeping;
- providing job references for students;
- involvement in Barlby/Brayton/Selby/Fulford planning consortium.

Role of the Curriculum Area Mentor

This member of staff will ensure that:

- the subject department works with the deputy and student teacher co-ordinator on all matters;

- the department is represented on the ITE sub-committee;
- students attend the subject induction session before under-taking their duties;
- students have a varied and balanced timetable;
- students attend departmental meetings;
- students are encouraged to perform a range of tasks within the department;
- written records of students' progress and performance are provided;
- support is offered to students in the form of regular planning and review discussions and opportunities to discuss wider educational issues relevant to the curriculum area;
- University curriculum tutors are fully involved in the department's supervision of student teachers;
- other members of the department are involved in monitoring and evaluating students' progress;
- class responses are monitored and action is taken to alleviate areas of difficulty;
- students are regularly observed in the classroom.

The final details of funding for 1993–94 arrived too late for planning sessions for curriculum area mentors to be allocated timetable time. Next year (1994/95) this will be planned in from the outset. This year (1993/94) departments have been allocated funding to use as appropriate, which could mean that they buy in supply cover (casual relief teachers) to create time for essential planning and preparation.

Thoughts about University staff not having time to support school staff and student teachers proved groundless. From the outset it was stated that the course would operate on a 2-day per week basis in Terms 1 and 3, on Tuesdays and Thursdays. One day, Tuesday, would focus on whole-school issues, such as pastoral care or class room management. The other day, Thursday, would be curriculum area day. On both days University tutors would be available for support. Regular visits by University tutors had been planned for each Tuesday as the Whole School Issues day was the area which caused greatest concern and uncertainty amongst school staff. The feeling was that while staff might be subject 'experts', they felt less confident about training students in the wider issues of the teachers' role. During Term 2 students were to be on full-time placement in schools, and staff felt much more assured of their competence to cope with a familiar situation, as the Spring Term classroom program remained virtually as it always had been. Again the University responded by ensuring that each student had three visits from a University tutor. These tutors were available to come in if further support was required at any time. In addition, once each term the University held meetings for all mentor teachers and curriculum area mentors. In all participating schools they placed a total of 180 students. The meetings at the University took the form of discussions of the program content and general discussion sessions with colleagues, and gave the opportunity to focus on items of concern. One further development from these meetings was the setting up of some groups of schools as mini-consortia to support each other further in the provision of the program. Fulford School worked with three other schools in the area and the resulting co-operative program expanded the experience of both students and teachers.

How were we to ensure that we were all looking for the same standards from the students? University tutors provided school staff with copies of the student profile, which was issued to all students. The profile sets out the specific criteria relating to professional competence, as stated by the Council for the Accreditation of Teacher Education (CATE). These profiles formed the basis of recording student achievement both by University staff and the students themselves. School teachers used these as guides for the work they were doing with students both in curriculum areas and the Whole School Issues course development. All formal reporting to the University was to be completed using the competences as the framework and criteria for comment.

We had frequently played host to large parties of foreign language students; some of the concern about numbers was based on the memories that the staff had of several large contingents, of student teachers around the school and the consequent difficulties. We do not have a particularly large staffroom, so that facilities such as working space, places to sit and coffee arrangements have been stretched beyond the limit on occasion. Staff were not happy with the thought that this could happen much more frequently with the presence of the student group in school for double the previous period of time. However, when it was made clear to staff that the school had set a limit on the number of students that would be taken, and that these students would work in departments whose staff were experienced in the training and support of students, the majority of colleagues were happy to proceed.

The matter of joint selection of students by school and University staff is to be addressed this year (1993/94). Most school colleagues feel that this is an area of involvement for schools and that we should have some say in the selection of students who will be undertaking two-thirds of their PGCE training in our schools.

At the outset the staff felt uncertain about the Whole School Issues program. Colleagues in schools were concerned that they might not have staff with the particular expertise required to run some of the sessions. The director published the Whole School Issues program setting out details of sessions and giving suggestions for possible in-school activities. This went a long way towards meeting the need for support and information. All PGCE students attended an initial lecture on Mondays at the University on the particular topic for that week, for example, communication skills and the use of language in the classroom. Brief details of these sessions were also distributed to schools. This gave school colleagues an outline to use in the planning and development of their own sessions. However, some of the topics chosen did not require a full day's program as follow-up; schools then had some flexibility to include sessions of particular interest to their own student group. For instance, many school professional tutors decided that it was essential to run further sessions on pastoral care, as students were generally rather worried about facing the demands of the form tutor role. The student view was that they were quite well prepared for their role as subject teachers, but they knew little about the activities of a form tutor and had little experience and limited skills to enable them to undertake the tasks with confidence. Student response to these additional sessions indicated some relief at being given the opportunity to discuss the issues and, in some cases, to meet colleagues from external agencies, who explained their role in terms of not only supporting the pupil with difficulties, but also working alongside form tutors as they attempted to help pupils.

Staffing of sessions would have been a thorny problem without the appointment of the coordinator and the full support of the head and senior management team. Colleagues, whose role in school meant that they would have particular expertise and experience to offer to students, were most helpful and often gave of their own time freely to prepare and run sessions.

A general problem is to ensure that planning information from the University is available to feed into the planning of the school timetable at an early stage. This means detailed planning at least six months ahead in order to ensure the release of requisite school staff. The creative efforts made at short notice in the first year have now been replaced by a carefully programmed timetable that allows the coordinator adequate planning and preparation time for the arrival of students.

At Fulford, the major responsibility for delivery of sessions still remains with the coordinator, but there is now more flexibility for other staff to participate. Increased resourcing from the University has 'bought' some supply teaching time to cover classes when required although this facility has been used sparingly in an attempt to avoid adversely affecting the educational experience of classes.

Releasing staff is a costly business and the significant increase in funding for the second year of the program has meant that not only will the appropriate staff be available for sessions, but money will be available for resources too. Programs of this type require resource books, materials, photocopying, stationery, transport, video and audio tapes. The program has now more appropriate levels of funding for these items, instead of borrowing from friendly departments as was the case in the start-up.

Another cost of our participation in ITE was the possible effect on our pupils of the increased presence of students in the classroom. The University gave clear information to all schools that the minimum teaching requirement for students in the first term was the team teaching of one lesson only. This helped to alleviate concern amongst staff about possible difficulties for pupils caused by new faces appearing more frequently in the classroom. The unsettling effects of a range of different staff for a particular class can be great because of lack of continuity of teaching styles. The usual class teacher was expected to play his/her part with the support of the head of department by helping students to plan and prepare sessions and to observe and debrief after sessions. This was important to ensure continuity of approach and progress of pupils during the first term as well as providing the essential mentor support for the students.

Although assessing practice was a task staff had previously undertaken when students were completing the full-time teaching placement, the plethora of instructions and information coming from a variety of different sources during the planning period gave rise to a clear request for a definitive list of the competences required from a student teacher. The Department of Educational Studies at The University of York made it clear that comments were to be based on the DfE competences (DfE 1992) of subject knowledge, subject application, class management, assessment and recording of pupils' progress and further professional development (see these in Chapter 1, p. 12). All University tutors used the same framework for comment and assessment that then allowed a clearer picture of the correlation between the assessment by University tutors and teachers and more effective reporting of student progress. Two reports were asked for by the University: for the full-time teaching placement students — one brief mid-term report was required to comment on the progress of students; this identified promptly the students whose performance in the classroom was causing concern. The summative report was a detailed account of the student's progress and development of the required competences. This was completed at the end of term. Comment on Terms 1 and 3 in-school program were less detailed as individual student input to school was at a much lower level on the two-day program. All staff working with students contributed to these reports. Information and comment was passed to the coordinator, whose responsibility it was to draw up the final reports which were then seen by the relevant staff and the students themselves before they were sent to the University. The purpose of this arrangement was to relieve staff of some of the burden of report writing and to involve the students in assessing their own performance, developing further the self-critical approach required of all teachers. The copies of the final report were then used as the basis for job references for students.

Fortunately, we have a former caretaker's house on campus which is now used for in-service training purposes and some music lessons. We established The House as the student base, where they had their own working area, meeting place, coffee supply and all other necessary facilities. This worked well as it helped to create a strong group identity and established a more informal approach during seminars and practical sessions which encouraged the quieter members of the group to contribute. This comparative informality enabled students to offer mutual support when things did not go as they had planned either in the classroom or with any of the activities in which they were involved. Also, the coordinator was seen to be available and approachable if any personal or professional problems needed another view. Larger scale exercises, such as the planning for the whole school multicultural education day benefited from the energy and input of the whole group from different subject disciplines. The students' being away from the main body of the school lessened interruptions and improved concentration on the tasks set. However, as we all wished the students to be seen as an integral part of the school from the outset, they were encouraged to participate in as many in-school activities as possible, to be seen on duty at breaks and lunchtimes and to be in the staffroom at particular breaks too.

In the end, the setting up and planning of the weekly sessions was reasonably straightforward after the groundwork of looking at staff concerns and attempts to find practical solutions to these difficulties had mostly been achieved.

What We Did

The program for the year was as follows:

Whole School Issues Program

1992/93 AUTUMN TERM	
Session 1	Communication skills and the use of language. Tutor: Head of English
Session 2	Discipline and classroom management. Tutor: Deputy Head, Year Head, Headteacher
Session 3	Meeting the needs of pupils with learning difficulties. Tutor: Special Needs Co-ordinator, support teachers
Session 4	The role of the form tutor, pastoral care and guidance and counselling. Tutor: Personal and Social Education Coordinator.
Session 5	Meeting the needs of more able pupils. Tutor: Special Needs Coordinator and Deputy Head
Session 6	Teaching personal and social education. Tutor: Personal and Social Education Coordinator
Session 7	Coping with the demands of teaching. Tutors: Brainstrust of beginning teachers; Headteacher: Head of Department; Year Head: Professor I. Lister, Head of Department of Educational Studies, University of York
NB. Personal and Social Education Coordinator and ITE Coordinator are the same person.	

Spring Term full-time teaching placement

LUNCHTIME SEMINAR PROGRAM	
Session 1	Departmental Induction. Tutors: Head of Department
Session 2	Whole school induction and identification of seminar program content. * Tutor: ITE Coordinator
Session 3	Personal and Social Education.
Session 4	Activities for tutorial time.
Session 5	Job Seeking Skills I. Tutor: Deputy Head
Session 6	Job Seeking Skills II. Tutor: Deputy Head
Session 7	Special needs provision.
Session 8	External agencies.
Session 9	Counselling pupils.
Session 10	All beginning teachers on school staff.
Session 11	Vocational education.
Session 12	End-of-term debrief.

* Tutor for remaining sessions not designated was the ITE Coordinator.

Whole School Issues Program

1993 — SUMMER TERM	
Session 1	The school as an organisation Tutor: Headteacher, School Governor, parent
Session 2	Providing equal opportunities and preparation for life in a multicultural society Tutor: ITE Coordinator
Session 3	Recording and reporting achievement Tutor: Deputy Head
Session 4	Careers education and guidance Tutor: Careers Coordinator, Careers Officer
Session 5	Health education, including sex education Tutor: Personal and Social Education Coordinator
Session 6	Environmental education Tutor: ITE Coordinators from 4 local schools
Session 7	Economic and industrial understanding Tutor: Head of Business Studies
Session 8	Staff appraisal and professional development Tutor: ITE Coordinators from local schools

The explanation in the University literature (PGCE Booklet 1992) of the school-based day and the role of the school is quoted below:

The aim of the school-based day is to explore each topic 'in practice'. As the context of each school varies so much between schools, we do not wish to be prescriptive about the type and nature of activities that should occur on the school-based days. These will be left to each school to decide for itself. However, we have listed a number of common aims for each school-based day together with some illustrative activities. Primarily, we would like the school to introduce students to an understanding of the key issues involved in each topic 'as faced by practitioners'. In addition, we would hope that where appropriate some activities could be devoted to developing the students' skills (for example through joint planning and teaching of a lesson, or discussion with a member of staff about how to respond to or deal with particular tasks or scenarios).

In this first year of operation of the development in the PGCE course, we are very conscious that both we and our school colleagues will be feeling our way. We do very much hope that this year's experience will prove to be valuable to all parties involved and will enable us to further develop the quality of the initial teacher training we jointly offer to students.

The booklet containing information on topics and illustrative activities for each session was sent out in response to requests for this support from school staff. An example of the session on 'The Role of the Form Tutor' is shown here:

PGCE AUTUMN TERM 1993

WHOLE SCHOOL ISSUES (Tuesdays)

Topics and illustrative activities

16th November: THE ROLE OF THE FORM TUTOR, PASTORAL CARE AND COUNSELLING

Aims:

To consider:

the nature of pastoral care;
the school's pastoral care structure and system;
the role of the form tutor;
the nature of pastoral care counselling.

Possible activities:

* Observation of registration or form period.

* Talk with a form tutor and head of pastoral care concerning pupil problems and their respective roles. Consider the pastoral care role of the classroom teacher.

* Prepare a tutor time activity in pairs and then review.

* Discuss some fictional case studies (e.g., a hard working low-attaining pupil under pressure from parents to do better and who

is worried about this and starts to truant without the parents' knowledge — what should be done?).

- In small groups make a list of the characteristics of a 'good' form tutor and then compare your lists. What types of concern should a classroom teacher draw to the attention of colleagues?

The Program in Detail

Autumn Term

The program began with a full day induction to the school; the purpose of this was to introduce student teachers to each other, to school staff and to allow the opportunity for the students to familiarise themselves with the physical layout of the school. A priority for the day was the involvement of the student teachers in an essential school issue from the outset. They were asked to examine litter problems and suggest possible constructive solutions. The reasons for this were three-fold:

- to encourage student teachers to feel that they had a valuable, contributing role to play in the school immediately;
- to create a situation where staff and pupils of the school could 'see' student teacher input and would feel that this group of newcomers was working to help overcome a problem of the whole school community;
- in the presentation of their solutions to the group at the end of the exercise to encourage student teachers to begin using essential classroom equipment, such as tape recorders, video camera, overhead projector and blackboard.

The program for the day ran as follows:

1	*Introductions:*	Headteacher, deputy head in charge of ITE and the ITE Coordinator
		Group introduction exercise
		********
2	*Administration:*	• information packs for each student
		• essential school procedures, such as arrival times, explanation of absences

- outline of program
- explanation of expected whole-school involvement for each student

****

3 *Treasure Hunt*
- a series of questions to answer by finding a variety of school locations, meeting teachers.

****

4 *Solve our litter problem*
- description by ITE Coordinator. 4 groups to investigate problem and then make a 10-minute presentation of their solution.

To encourage students to develop a detailed understanding of the range of roles a teacher must fulfil other than classroom teaching responsibility, all students were informed that they were expected to perform several other tasks for the school from the outset of the course in addition to their full involvement in the 2-day program. The tasks were chosen to reflect the pastoral, departmental and whole school involvement required of members of the profession. Students were asked:

- to work with a form tutor;
- to do duties with this form tutor;
- to attend/run an extra-curricular activity;
- to attend/participate in school assemblies;
- to attend year meetings, staff meetings, department meetings;
- to attend all meetings with the professional tutor;
- to work alongside midday supervisory assistants.

The Feedback Session

The Treasure Hunt had helped student teachers to work together and get to know each other. They had met a large number of staff and found their way to the furthermost reaches of the campus. The exercise had helped everyone to overcome the nervousness associated with coping with a new situation.

The feedback on the litter exercise was very lively. Ideas ranged from buying more litter bins and relocating existing bins, through various competitions, to the positive approach of setting up the Green Club. This Club was ultimately to focus on wider environmental issues, but the starting point was the school environment and a full scale anti-litter campaign run by pupils that was supported by the student teachers. The Green Club was the chosen strategy of the whole group. The Headteacher was present throughout the session and he was particularly keen on this approach, which helped the group to feel confident when beginning the task.

Student teachers then planned and ran assemblies for all year groups to publicise Green Club and its campaign. Pupils responded well to the imaginative presentations and eventually two Year 10 girls and the student teachers ran the club. It has since made an effective contribution to the improvement of the school environment. Detailed examples of the programs for the Whole School Issues day are listed below:

COMMUNICATION SKILLS AND THE USE OF LANGUAGE

1   Use of language in the classroom — theoretical input from head of English, followed by several language exercises.

2   Classroom observation sessions — student teachers to observe lessons in two academic subjects other than their own specialist area and one practical subject. The task was to observe and note different types of language used and differing styles of communication.

3   School Communication looking at:
    • communications with parents
    • general in-school communication, such as notice boards and displays
    • staff communication
    • policy documents
    Groups chose one aspect of communication and reviewed materials. Written comments for improvement were required.

4   Each student teacher was attached to a midday supervisory assistant to help them observe pupil-to-pupil and supervisor-pupil communication in the playground.

5   Review of observed styles of communication and assessment of effective communication.

DISCIPLINE AND CLASSROOM MANAGEMENT

1   Headteacher, deputy head and head of department input on policy and practice, differing roles and responsibilities. Also 'What to do when . . .'

2 Classroom observation of three different classroom sessions. Completion of observation schedules.

3 Seminar with year heads — 'What to look for in a well-managed classroom'

4 Review session using observation schedules. 'What you observed which constitutes good/bad classroom managements? Why are some approaches more effective than others?'

MEETING THE NEEDS OF PUPILS WITH LEARNING DIFFICULTIES

1 Seminar with Coordinator of Special Needs — school and county policy.

2 Students to work with pupils in special needs base alongside support staff.

3 Review of materials and preparation of own differentiated materials for curriculum area supported by coordinator. (These materials to be used for first team teaching session in curriculum area).

4 Student teachers to take a Year 9 cognitive abilities test — to have a close look at what is required of pupils.

5 Beginning teachers panel to speak about 'Coping with mixed ability classes'.

Throughout the year curriculum area days were based on the accepted model of planning and preparation of materials for lessons, team teaching of some sessions with one other student and review of the session with the subject mentor teacher and head of department. Links between the Whole School Issues days and curriculum area work were essential, if student teachers were to be encouraged to reflect on the breadth of the demands of the teaching role. The Whole School Issues session offered time for them to develop their skills, for example, in the production of differentiated materials in preparation for their team teaching. The active support of staff with the expertise not only to show the student teachers how to produce materials matched to the age, ability and attainment levels of pupils, but also to encourage and support reflection on the issues involved in the task was essential for the successful completion of the exercise.

A new, different group of student teachers joined the school for their full-time teaching placement in the second term, as experience working in more than one school is required in the DES guidelines for initial teacher education (DES 1989).

Spring Term

The content of the program for the Spring Term has been described earlier. However, in addition to this new seminar program, we thought it essential to continue to develop student teacher understanding of their whole-school role. To this end, they were expected to follow the same program of involvement as the first term students in the pastoral, academic and extra-curricular work of the school. We found that student experience of these areas from the Autumn Term sessions in other schools did vary, and in one particular case this was, in part, responsible for the significant lack of confidence of one student. By involving all student teachers and starting them all with the same range of tasks it was felt this might help to overcome the discrepancies of experience. In addition, all students were given the choice of becoming involved in subject areas other than their specialist subject. Consequently to give an overview of the functioning of the school, we had English students teaching Textiles, Foreign Language students working on Vocational courses and Science students supporting Music lessons. The purpose of this was to broaden student understanding of the classroom process and increase their perception of what happens elsewhere in school. These sessions were very popular with both school staff and student teachers. Vocational students in one session benefited from all the student teachers running mock interviews for them as practice before their interviews for further education courses. The student teachers also gained confidence by practising their interviewing skills. This also helped to point up the value and relevance of University sessions on communication skills. Student teacher feedback on such sessions was entirely positive. Comments such as:

> It's good to see for oneself exactly what happens in Careers lessons/Textiles lessons — it's very interesting to see how differently pupils behave in other classroom environments.

> Children who I've seen achieving very little in my lessons obviously have other talents. It was good to see.

> I've always wondered what Food Technology was. I really enjoyed myself, but isn't it scientific?

Summer Term

By the time we were preparing the Summer Term program, confidence amongst the mentor teachers was growing. Positive feedback on the Autumn program from students helped us feel that our approach and the content of sessions had been relevant to the needs and development of the student teacher group.

This response was general amongst staff in most partnership schools and gave rise to an increasingly inventive approach. Some schools formed local consortia for planning and provision of the course. The expert in appraisal in one school ran a full-day program for student teachers attached to three other schools as well as his own. Another session on Environmental Education was planned and run by the student teachers in the same four schools. The purpose of the day was for the student teachers to plan, prepare and use materials for their own curriculum areas based on environmental issues. The breadth of experience and expertise in the large group resulted in a most challenging review of the activities, and positive support was given to all participants as they were all facing their most critical audience — themselves. The wide exchange of ideas meant students spent a considerable time asking for examples of each other's work. The mentor teachers' role in all this was to provide the necessary background information on the issues in environmental education for schools and from that point to support and encourage group work on these issues. They joined in the student teacher review session, but encouragement of reflection was not necessary; it went on until the session ran over time.

The final term demanded more of the mentor teachers in terms of offering individual support to student teachers who had to cope with a wide variety of pressures. Assessment tasks had to be completed for the University; applications for jobs took a considerable amount of time and often students who were asked for job interviews were not present at a session. Anxiety levels were high and valuable time was spent by mentors with students preparing and debriefing them for job interviews. Comprehensive previous experience of being required to reflect critically on their own performance was felt by the students to have given them a sound basis for coping with job interviews.

The difficulties lay, for the Summer Term, rather ironically, in the success of the students' Autumn Term experience which had considerably developed their confidence and ability to cope with full-time school experience. The majority who had positive experiences in the second term were then frustrated by the restrictions of the return to the two-day program. They had taken on a great deal of responsibility for their own work, had their own classes and had also become contributing members of the staff team in the previous term. The return to the University and their Autumn-term schools after Easter was therefore particularly frustrating. This was a time when the mentor had to respond to their expressed concerns to enable their professional development to continue rather than letting them falter at such a crucial point. Listening to and accepting their views were vital, but immediate action was essential to retain student confidence. The University had established that some flexibility was essential to the success of the program and this was the time to act and adapt the planned program. Student teachers at Fulford School were asked what other experiences would best encourage their further professional development at this time. They identified the following areas:

- Information Technology;
- timetabling skills;
- working with children with special educational needs;
- vocational education;
- teaching personal and social education;
- library review of materials for curriculum area;
- shadowing a deputy head;
- shadowing a head of department.

Several of these choices indicated ideas of future career paths, others were requested in order to meet more immediate needs for experience in areas of uncertainty for particular members of the group. The responsibility for the organisation, timing and negotiations for the setting up of these sessions was handed over to the student teachers, answering in part, their need to feel some control over their time in school. The mentor teacher's input to these proceedings was to sound out the colleagues, who would be involved in the provision of these sessions, to help to ensure a positive response for student teachers' requests. This role of student teacher advocate is central to the new role of the mentor teacher. The principle of allowing the students to choose the topic for, and run, certain sessions helped to increase student commitment at a time when they were looking outward towards their future jobs. This is an approach which it would be helpful to build on for this Summer Term program next year.

The University and schools undertook evaluation of the course with the student teachers. Comments were helpful and the content of part of the course for next year has been altered in response to requests for an even broader view of the role of the teacher.

The Future

At York much of the structure offered by the University to partnership schools and the training of mentor teachers will be retained for the next academic year. However, the increasing transfer of resources to schools has affected the level of staffing of the Department of Educational Studies at the University. The inevitable knock-on effect of this will be a reduction in University tutor in-school support. Mentor teachers and subject mentors will still attend meetings with University tutors to discuss issues and plan the program. However, schools will now have more responsibility for the implementation, staffing and resourcing of their own programs as well as assessment of student teachers' competence. As mentor teachers take on increasing responsibilities, much could be lost for the professional development of student teachers if they were to base their school initial teacher education programs entirely on the required competences established by CATE. The particular demands of teaching different subjects and developing the wide range of strengths and approaches of individual teachers require a broader view of the provision of programs, which must inform, challenge and develop student teachers to a level of proficiency that allows them to begin their career in teaching with confidence and competence.

In the programs of training, mentor teachers must also work to achieve a balance between the necessary complementary role of school sessions in support of work done by student teachers at the University and the encouragement of the development of the individual talents of the student teachers in their schools.

The basic skills and tasks of the mentor, such as the provision and teaching of a program of learning which develops the understanding and knowledge of the teaching role and liaison with Higher Education Institutions to ensure parity of experience for students, remain the same. An additional and different role is now apparent. During the last year, competition for student teacher places in schools has, in some areas, become quite strong, and financial packages offered to schools vary between institutions. The mentor teacher in many schools has had to take on the role of negotiator, as resource levels per student teacher can vary widely.

This, in turn, had identified further issues for mentors. As the role is, of necessity, changing to respond to new demands, time and support are required to allow mentors to reflect on their practice and to plan strategies for coping with these extra responsibilities. In-service training opportunities are growing, but materials for training are only just becoming available in schools. We have found that working with colleagues in other schools has been a most constructive experience and it has allowed some time for reflection as well as planning. Comments from members of the group of mentor teachers at Fulford School indicate a high level of commitment and job satisfaction, as well as a strong feeling that they have learned much from observing fresh and different approaches to teaching. Our pupils can only benefit from this interchange between student teachers and their mentors.

Chapter 7

Integrating Theory and Practice in Teacher Education: the UEA Model of Action-research Based Teacher Education

Chris Husbands

Introduction: Models of 'School-Based' Teacher Education

In many important respects, initial teacher education has, of course, *always* been school-based; students have learned to teach in classrooms with pupils and they have been supported in doing so, albeit frequently informally, by teachers in placement schools (Alexander 1984; Bell 1981; Gardner 1993). In this sense, the use of the term 'school-based teacher education' to describe the enhancement of the roles of teachers and schools in initial or pre-service teacher education is a misnomer, which tends to focus excessively on the proportions of time spent by students in classrooms, or school, rather than on the re-conceptualisation and clarification of roles in initial teacher education which lies at the heart of current models of competency-based or school-focused teacher education (Booth 1993; Zeichner 1990). There is, in consequence, no clear consensus about the nature of school-based teacher education, and recent research and knowledge on the nature of school-based teacher education would support a variety of models (McIntyre 1987; Furlong *et al.* 1988; Lawlor 1990). In some versions, 'school-based' teacher education is used in general terms to describe higher-education based models which make particular and extensive use of particular relationships with schools; in others it is used in an ideologically-driven way to describe models which exclude the participation of higher education (Lawlor 1990; O'Heare 1988); and in yet other versions, it is used to describe 'school-led' models of training which describe a market relationship between schools and higher education (Beardon *et al.* 1992). For this reason, many teacher educators eschew the phrase 'school-based teacher education', as lacking precision, clarity and utility, using instead concepts such as 'internship' (Oxford), or 'partnership-based teacher education' (East Anglia).

The purpose of this chapter is to describe a model of competency-based, school-focused teacher education under development at the University of East Anglia (UEA) before national policy developments in early 1992, though accelerated by those developments. It does so by setting in context current thinking on the roles of schools in teacher education and by outlining the planning basis and structure of the UEA program, demonstrating ways in which a teacher education curriculum is built by relating theoretical research-based conclusions about professional learning and practical traditions of partnership between schools and higher education.

Recent attempts to clarify the roles of Higher Education Institutions and school teachers in working with student teachers have derived from a number of sources. The development in the middle and later 1980s of the Oxford internship model of teacher education was based on the conviction that:

> any school of education can demonstrate the sincerity of its respect for the practitioner by committing major tasks of training to him [*sic*]. (Judge 1980: 47)

However, McIntyre notes that research evidence from conventional models of initial teacher education demonstrates that:

> student-teachers generally do not learn much although there is a great deal to be learned, from . . . experienced teachers . . . because the(y) do not know what to look for and because the teachers often do not recognise how much there is to be learned from their own teaching. (McIntyre 1987: 105)

In consequence, the fundamental elements of the Oxford internship were the development of a framework which shared the responsibility for initial teacher education between the Oxford Department of Educational Studies and a relatively small number of schools each playing host to a relatively large number of students or interns — up to twelve per school. The Oxford internship program was developed between 1987 and 1990 by teams of Oxford University Department of Education Studies (OUDES) tutors and seconded teachers, and the subsequent management of the scheme was shared between the University and the participating schools (Pendry 1990). Within the school, the key feature of the internship was that each intern:

[had] a secure personal relationship with a mentor . . . being accepted in [school] departments not as fleeting visitors but as members of these departments for the whole school year [of the PGCE]. (McIntyre 1987: 107)

Considerable time and energy were then invested in the development of curriculum and support structures which both allowed interns to access the professional craft knowledge of their mentors and which supported mentors in the articulation of their own practice in school-based work with interns (McIntyre and Hagger 1993).

A second significant collection of research findings of the later 1980s generated what has been called the Cambridge Analytical Framework (Furlong *et al.* 1988; McIntyre 1990). The Cambridge team studied four school-based initial teacher training programs in detail, seeking to clarify the role of the school in developing student competence in each program. They identified four levels or dimensions of professional training:

Level [a] Direct practice . . . involv[ing] the development of understanding judgement, and skills through direct practical experience in the classroom. . . . Understanding, judgement and skills are here essentially acquired by students in immediate, first-hand experience; issues of professional principle and theory are entirely implicit . . .

Level [b] Indirect practice . . . concerns the acquisition of practical understanding, judgement and skills but in detached contexts rather than through direct practical experience. Once again issues of theory and principle are implicit. Taken together Levels [a] and [b] may also be used as a basis for more principled and theoretical forms of training addressed at Levels [c] and [d].

Level [c] involves the acquisition of knowledge of the principles behind different professional practices and reflection on their use and justification. . . .

Work at Level [d] is of a different order in that its purpose is to make explicit and critically examine . . . value judgements and theoretical assumptions by reference to the foundation disciplines of education (Furlong *et al.* 1988: 129–31).

The Cambridge model went on to argue that in terms of the partnerships between Higher Education Institutions and schools, Level [a] work was exclusively the concern of school teachers who 'have the direct knowledge and experience of the classes with which students will be involved', whilst Level [d] work 'can in general only be carried out by lecturers' (Furlong *et al.* 1988: 206–7). Levels [b] and [c] could become the province of schoolteachers, 'through some form of in-service training to develop the explicit use of the necessary analytical and critical skills of working with students' (Furlong *et al.* 1988: 207). The Cambridge model has been criticised for its over-schematic characterisation of teacher education (for example, McIntyre 1990), and it further appears to rely heavily on Hirst's description of the knowledge-base of teaching, characterising the levels of professional learning in terms of knowledge and understanding (Hirst 1983; but also see Elliott 1991). However, taken together, the Oxford internship and the Cambridge analytical framework have contributed considerably to understandings of the nature of teachers' professional learning and to a clarification of the potential role of schools in initial teacher education. An extensive literature on mentoring has developed, and by 1992, a quarter of Higher Education Institutions used the label for teachers' contributing to initial teacher education (Whitty *et al.* 1992: 302).

At the same time, there was a variety of developments and local initiatives in teacher education. Such developments had a number of broad characteristics. The first was an enhancement of the role of the school in initial teacher education both within traditional PGCE routes to qualified teacher status (Everton and White 1992; Husbands 1993; Goodfellow 1992; Barrett *et al.* 1992a), and through the development of novel, more intensively school-based routes to Qualified Teacher Status (QTS) through the licensed and articled teacher schemes (Barrett *et al.* 1992b). By 1991, most students on traditional PGCE courses were based in schools for in excess of 50 per cent and sometimes 60 per cent or 66 per cent of their time, whilst those on two-year articled teacher programs were based in schools for 80 per cent of their course. At the same time the profiling of student teachers was widely adopted as an assessment and monitoring component of initial teacher education programs, which helped focus attention on the processes of learning to teach and the exit competences which newly-qualified teachers might be expected to demonstrate (Husbands 1993; Beardon *et al.* 1992; Vaughan 1992; Whitty and Willmott 1991). Taken together with the Oxford internship and the Cambridge analytical framework, such developments had laid considerable experiential and conceptual groundwork for responses to the development of national policy in respect of teacher education. The effect of the publication of revised criteria for the accreditation of courses of teacher education requiring all secondary

PGCE students to be based in school for a minimum of 24 weeks of their 36-week course, and transferring the assessment of student teachers onto a competency-based model was to further stimulate discussion between schools and Higher Education Institutions (DfE 1992; CATE 1992).

The Development of an Action-Research Model of Teacher Education at the University of East Anglia

This section describes a model of teacher education within the framework of a one-year post-graduate program developed at the University of East Anglia between 1991 and 1993, built on the research and information base generated by the Oxford and Cambridge frameworks and parallel developments in teacher education outlined above. Discussions on developing initial teacher education in the region, as a response to some of the structural difficulties of traditional PGCE courses had taken place throughout the 1980s and produced a number of small-scale innovations (Brown 1985; Halliwell 1988), but were accelerated in the Autumn of 1991 and Spring of 1992, a time of rapid change in teacher education, as school-focused, competency-led models of initial teacher education were established in national policy (Clarke 1992; DfE 1992).

The Schools

Certain features and traditions of East Anglia and of the University School of Education were highly influential in the planning of curriculum models for initial teacher education against the current research and national policy backgrounds. Most secondary schools in East Anglia, outside the two major urban areas of Norwich and Ipswich, are relatively small (500–750 pupils); the pattern of 11–16, 12–16, 13–18, 11–19 and 16–19 institutions is complex, which creates difficulties in planning student experience across the entire secondary age range. Headteachers were concerned that the model of initial teacher education adopted should not overload their schools. In these schools, faculty rather than departmental structures are common and many teachers teach across a number of cognate disciplines. Headteachers further argued that the development of school-focused initial teacher education should not, by default, exclude any schools or types of schools from participation in the professional preparation of student teachers, but that both rural and urban schools, both large and small schools had a distinctive part to play in initial teacher education. In particular, the strong pressures within the emerging national policy models for the concentration of initial teacher education in relatively few, larger, schools was seen as a divisive implication of policy development, which discriminated against smaller schools. Such factors inhibited the development and adoption of an internship model of teacher education.

The School of Education and Action Research

Within the University of East Anglia's School of Education the tradition of action-research and, in particular, the conceptualisation of professional development as grounded in systematic workplace enquiry, was well established. The work of Stenhouse and his advocacy of the teacher-as-researcher (Stenhouse 1975), together with John Elliott's influential leadership of the action research movement (Elliott 1990) ensured that action research has for some time played a central role in the thinking of the School of Education at the University of East Anglia and in award-bearing, in-service provision (Elliott 1985). A considerable number of teachers in secondary schools in the region have undertaken in-service work at the University, and the concept of action research is well developed in many schools in the region. Some of the implications are developed by Elliott in characterising a *practical science* model of teacher education. Elliott distinguishes between what he calls *habitual skill action* and what he calls *intelligent skill action*. Teaching is characterised by Elliott as intelligent skill action, and:

> Teacher education . . . is largely a matter of developing a teacher's capacities for situational understandings as a basis for wise judgement and intelligent decisions in complex, ambiguous and dynamic educational situations. (Elliott 1991:7)

This intellectual tradition disposed both the University and schools against apprenticeship models of initial training and against reductive interpretations of competency-based frameworks. At the same time, the action-research tradition has generated a particular view of the relationship between theory and practice and, in particular, on the grounded nature of theoretical reflection which focuses attention particularly closely on the development of conceptual, curricular and administrative frameworks which would allow teachers, students and higher education tutors to integrate effectively the four dimensions of the Cambridge framework.

The Practice

The strength of action-research traditions in the University and its neighbour schools provided a promising starting point for the development of school-based training for both schools and the University. Indeed, early work with Headteachers suggested that they were strongly disposed towards developing school-based initial teacher education as far as possible within an action-research framework, grounded in the structured observation and investigation of classroom practice, in which the school is both the setting for classroom practice and the location of professional investigation. The program of initial teacher education developed between the University and its regional schools reflects this shared concern. The planning base for the program (see Figure 4) is generated by three related ideas about students' learning in schools.

How Student Teachers Learn in Schools (1)

Student teachers learn to teach by developing their ideas about teaching in specific contexts: '. . . learning to teach must be a continual process of hypothesis testing' (Alexander 1984). It is entirely possible to develop a teacher education curriculum from such a starting point within the framework of a competency-based accreditation and assessment framework (DfE 1992). The fundamental task in any school-focused teacher education curriculum is that of establishing integration between school and University components. A variety of research evidence suggests that in conventional models of teacher education there are sharp disjunctions between a student's experience in the University and in schools: schools and Universities tacitly disagree about the aims of teaching practice; schools are unable to provide a coherent, learning-focused experience for students; student experiences may be contingent on the whims of supervising teachers (Alexander 1984; McIntyre 1987; and see Chapter 3). The UEA model is based on extensive dialogue between schools and the University at the level of aims, purposes and principles, and the desire for an action-research, hypothesis testing approach emerged not from the University but from schools. The UEA program grounds this hypothesis testing in the observation and analysis of specific departments, and in the systematic observation of a student's placement partner. From the beginning of the program, classroom-based hypothesis-generation and development lie at the core of student learning since 'the classroom is not only a place of work but also a source of professional development' (Thiessen 1992:86). Teacher learning is not straightforward (Calderhead 1987), and teachers do not develop . . . by themselves . . . (T)hey learn most, perhaps from other teachers, particularly from colleagues in the workplace, their own school. (But) there is no simple way for teachers to learn from their colleagues. (Hargreaves 1992)

The following are the essential features of the UEA school-based practice teaching sessions.

- Unlike the learning in the Oxford internship program (McIntyre 1987:98–9) student learning is not centred on one school, but on two after an initial period of school observation: one in the first half of the year, and one in the second half of the year, although the distribution of block and serial placement between the two schools varies (Figure 4). There are strictly practical reasons for this maximal interpretation of the guidance accompanying the DfE criteria for secondary training (CATE 1992), which relate to the Headteachers' concerns that their relatively small schools and small departments should not be overloaded with students;

- Student teachers begin attachment to a placement school within a few days of registering on the PGCE program, and early school-located experience is heavily weighted towards structured observation in which the institution-based and school-located elements of the program mesh by focusing on particular disaggregated elements of teaching;

- Each student teacher has another student teacher with whom to share responsibilities, observations and problems;

- Schools, students and the University exploit the potential of paired placements to the full in order to generate team teaching, observation of experienced classroom teachers and of each other;

- Early in the program, student teachers undertake few teaching activities, and subsequently induction to teaching is structured and progressive. Early teaching is therefore grounded in a variety of activities which focus attention clearly on the task of providing opportunities to learn: small group and individual work; observation of individual pupils and of teachers; the collation of a bank of observation and evaluation data in the form of a learning journal;

- The first six weeks of the program, during which student teachers are attached to placement schools for two days a week, and to the University for three days a week provide the basis for this dissection of teaching;

- Student teachers are expected to begin teaching a small group of students on a regular basis from the third week of the program; they are expected to teach a whole class before the beginning of their block placement; and they are encouraged to see the transition in the seventh week of the taught program to full block placement in their school as relatively insignificant. They will have taught in the school before the beginning of block placement and should continue to observe pupils and teachers, to work with small groups of students, and to team teach after the beginning of the block placement;

- At the same time, the grounding of early learning in practice acknowledges that student teachers' early needs may predominantly involve, 'looking to the mentor to provide quick and effective access to the recipes which will make him or her a member of the profession' (Booth 1993:196, following Schutz 1971), though this is a preliminary stage only;

- Some commentators on competency-based frameworks for teacher education have warned against the possible atomisation of elements of teaching (Whitty and Willmott 1992). However, for student teachers to operate effectively as professional learners, some disaggregation of the components of teaching is essential. Others, such as, Macdonald 1984; Munro 1989, have suggested that student teachers confuse the deployment of coping strategies in the classroom with the deployment of effective teaching techniques. The essential early feature, therefore, is to ensure that student teachers focus on the classroom as a learning environment and that they focus on those features of teacher activity (questioning, management of learning, deployment of a range of resources) which provide opportunities to learn (Woods 1990);

- The central difficulty, as Brown and McIntyre (1986:36) point out, is that teachers' knowledge of their own practice is embedded in teachers' everyday actions in the classroom, and seldom made explicit. If new student teachers are to gain access to this knowledge, their induction to it needs to be carefully structured so that the implicit becomes explicit. Observation of practice, linked to a program of development, analysis and reflection in higher education continues throughout the course, but student teachers' own practice plays an increasingly important role;

- Just as observation is structured, so is practice: team-teaching, small-group teaching, support teaching and whole-class teaching all play important parts. Student teachers' learning from practice is supported in several ways: through their observation of, and work with, experienced teachers in school; through their observation of, and work with their subject partner in the school; and through their analysis of and reflection on their own practice in support-teaching, small-group and whole class work.

How Student Teachers Learn in Schools (2)

The second basis of the UEA school-based practice teaching program is a conception of teaching as a research-based, reflective activity, in which observation, practice and research are closely linked (Stenhouse 1975:ch. 10).

Student teachers' first block placement (a term which we prefer to the more usual label of teaching practice or *practicum*) lasts for five weeks and ends at the end of the first school term (see Figure 4). The focus for both student teachers and co-tutors at this stage is on the development of a range of practical teaching skills which draw on the focus on learning in the first six weeks. For co-tutors and for students, review and observation guidance provides a structure which emphasises the diagnosis of strengths and weaknesses and the setting of targets in one of six defined areas of effective teaching.

In many programs of initial teacher education, the end of block school experience concludes student teachers' relationships with their schools. In the UEA program, however, students return to their first placement school for a further five weeks of two-day per week placement. There are a number of reasons for this. The ending of placement with the ending of block practice tends to encourage students to think in terms of survival to the end of term/placement. It focuses student teachers' attentions on the achievement of short term goals. It produces sharp discontinuities for students in developing a progressive acquisition of skills and understandings. It makes attention to diagnosed strengths and weaknesses difficult to deploy and produces difficulties

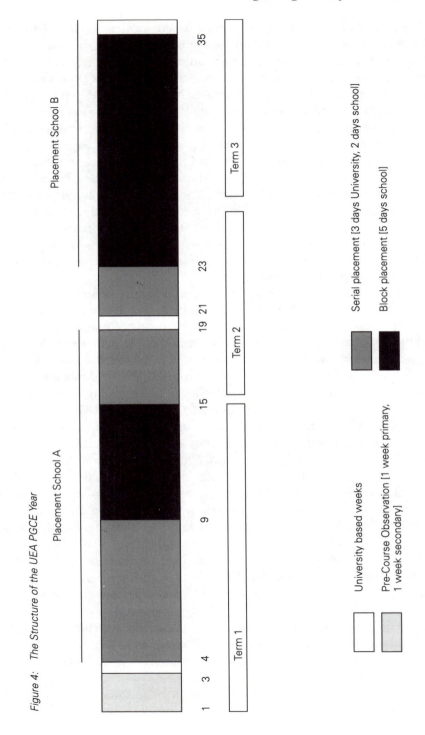

Figure 4: The Structure of the UEA PGCE Year

for effective target setting. In school-based models of initial teacher education, moreover, it tends to vest power over the program in the hands of, for example, the Higher Education Institution managing the overall coherence of the program since only the higher education tutor has access to the different contexts of training. More positively, the return to the first placement school enables students to explore educational issues in a context which they have now experienced in two different ways: as learners (on serial placement) and as teachers (on block placement); it creates continuing dialogue between co-tutor and student teacher and it encourages both parties to see their commitment to each other in longer-term context. The second term serial placement therefore provides an opportunity for a range of activities in relation to students' own learning needs. Students are likely to continue to teach. They are likely to continue to work with small groups of pupils and with individuals and to observe, now in more highly-focused and specific terms, experienced teachers.

In addition, during this period, a central feature of student teachers' programs is the school-based research project which students undertake in pairs after they have completed a period of both serial attachment and block placement in a school. The timing and structure of the project are both important. In so far as it is possible within the constraints of the one-year initial teacher education program, the students are by this time insider-researchers, with an implicit understanding of the institution in which they have been placed (Elliott 1990). These research projects build into the program some important ideas about school development and student learning; they may address classroom issues [for example, pupils talk in a particular subject] curriculum specific issues (for example, how pupils with learning difficulties respond to the school's science curriculum), or whole-school issues (such as gender influences on the school's 14+ options system), but the important idea is of the school 'commissioning' and learning from research into its own practices whilst the students are establishing ways of learning about and developing practice. At the level of 'embedded activity' in teaching (Brown and McIntyre 1986), this is another way of providing students with access into schools' and teachers' implicit assumptions about practice.

At the mid-point of the year, student teachers conclude their practice in their first placement school, and move to a second school (see Figure 4). Ideally, this second school will itself have been host to students in the same subject for the first half of the year, but such a closely integrated model is not always possible, for the same reasons as precluded the development of an internship model.

The serial placement in the second school is much shorter; the focus is less on observation and rather more on induction into the procedures of the school. This is a period of rapid learning for students: a series of contextualised understandings about the way in which educational institutions are organised and operate has been built up over the first half of the year and in one school. These understandings need to be reappraised in a new setting. It may be that a longer induction period would be more helpful, but the constraints of time and of *Circular 9/92* make that an unaffordable luxury. Coherence and continuity of student experience across a multi-site training program are critically important. In the UEA model, they are largely established through the Record of Student Experience (RoSE) — (cf. RoAD in Chapter 5 and RoPA in Chapter 8) — which constitutes the main information system in the program, and which was developed collaboratively between the University and schools, through course-development teams of University tutors and school teachers which have designed the structure of the program, written detailed guidance on curriculum structure and assessment and, in working groups, developed the detailed distribution of themes and activities throughout the year and between school and higher education.

Co-tutors in the second school have access to notes on the student teachers' targets and on reviews of teaching during the first placement in the RoSE, so that while students are new to the second school, there is a basis of information for both students and co-tutors.

The emphasis on second placement is more intensively on students as teachers, teaching up to a 75 per cent timetable. Guidance to student teachers and schools, however, makes it plain that observation and interrogation of the practice of experienced teachers is as valid at the end of the program as it is at the beginning of the program. While the agenda of observation may have altered, and the balance between practice and observation may have shifted, the principles of observation remain valid. The precise shape of each student's experience in this second school is likely to depend on the diagnosis of learning needs agreed with the second school co-tutor on the basis of the RoSE and on the experiences which the school is able to offer.

How Student Teachers Learn in Schools (3)

The third planning basis underpinning the UEA school-based teacher education program is that since teaching is a research-based, reflective activity, any separation of theory and practice between schools and the

University is untenable, as both are equally concerned with practice and theory (Elliott 1991). Thus schools are the location for practice, but they are also places where practice is interrogated by student teachers and by teachers working together.

The guidance on observation and review of students' teaching produced by the University and a group of Deputy Headteachers takes the form of a series of 'prompt' questions. During student teachers' first placement, as a part of their submission for formal assessment, they compile a learning journal, an analytical dossier of observations and reflections on their own practice, their partner's practice and the practice of experienced teachers.

Schools, however, are also places which interrogate and develop their own practice. The second-term school-based research project is on a theme arising from the development plan of the students' placement school. This project is agreed in negotiation between student teachers and the school and supervised not from the University but from the school. The University is equally concerned with both practice and the investigation of practice: the agreed course is organised through a series of questions about classroom practice, whole school-policy and schooling. The core of the program is practice as observed and experienced by the students in their placement schools.

The central task of the University programs is to help student teachers to develop their understanding of, and facility in, classroom practice through accessing experienced teachers' craft knowledge (Brown and McIntyre 1986) and, increasingly, an understanding of curriculum through processes of school development planning (Hargreaves and Hopkins 1991).

Teacher education is therefore a matter of supporting student teachers' access into, and teachers' articulation of the professional craft knowledge of teaching. In this sense 'theory' is an inappropriate term to describe the concerns of higher education: the concern of the higher education component of the program is with the investigation, analysis and refinement of classroom practice through case study and observation, and the task of teacher educators in the development of practice through a course philosophy and course structure which places a view of practice as 'intelligent skill action' at its core (Elliott 1991).

Conclusions

It is clear that no teacher education curriculum can be designed without a clear conception of the model of teaching on which it is based and towards which it points. Some commentators (Whitty and Willmott 1991) have warned that the imposition of competency-based frameworks on teacher education runs the risk of narrowing conceptions of teaching to the observation and imitation of workplace skills. In exploring the framework of national policy on teacher education, we have found alternative conceptions of teaching, drawing on intellectual traditions and professional practice within East Anglia, which are at least as useful in framing an initial teacher education curriculum. In this sense, the competencies of *Circular 9/92* and the opportunities to clarify the contribution of the school to initial teacher education have provided opportunities to extend and widen a critical discourse between Higher Education Institutions and schools about what teacher education is for, and what sort of teaching we are jointly committed to developing.

In addition, there are fundamental difficulties involved in describing a teacher education program through the structure of the program and the course components which it contains. If learning to teach is a process inadequately described by the enumeration of exit competencies, it is equally inadequately described by the analysis of the structure of student teacher experience in the program. Learning to teach occurs in classrooms, where new teachers explore their own understandings of teaching and learning in the light of experience and the context in which they are operating. McIntyre has argued (1987) that at the centre of initial teacher education is a process of transformation which can only begin by building on new teachers' own ideas about teaching and learning. For this reason, the important elements of the UEA program are the opportunities it provides for the development of professional learning relationships between co-tutors and student teachers, between student teachers and their partners and between higher education tutors and co-tutors and student teachers. What remains open, of course, is the extent to which these relationships provide opportunities for new teachers to develop competence and confidence in their most important relationships, with young people in schools.

Critical issues, then, remain. Not the least of these is the establishment of criteria by which school-based, competency-determined training should, in the medium term, be evaluated at a time when routes into teaching are becoming increasingly diverse (Wilkin 1993:320). Teacher educators have rightly laid considerable stress on the importance of evaluation, and particularly on internal evaluation based on feedback from students about effective and less effective parts of their program. Such evaluation has typically been straightforward since the teacher education curriculum being evaluated has been an internally coherent, institutionally-based curriculum. Models such as the Oxford internship

Chris Husbands

and the UEA model described here provide more complex programs for evaluation. Student teacher experience is more diffuse, scattered between different locations. The maintenance of an overview of student experience is consequently more problematic. Ownership of the program is less easy to define in terms of practical accountability. Such problems underpin some highly critical accounts of current policy initiatives in teacher education (see Gilroy 1992). However, the explicit concerns with the nature of the relationship between teachers and higher education-based teacher educators has foregrounded a series of problems which have been endemic in teacher education (McIntyre 1992:105–6). Internal audits of student experience, the incorporation of student evaluation in forward planning and the establishment by higher education of agreed programs of evaluation will remain important. At the heart of the evaluation of partnership-based teacher education, however, must be an explicit concern with the quality of communication between different partners, with the management of student teacher learning and with the purposes of different components of student teacher programs in the development of new teachers' confidence, skill and competence. It should be a highly productive, if problematic, dialogue.

Chapter 8

The Mentoring Scheme of Warwick University and Its School Partners — One Year On

Martin Robinson

Introduction

This chapter is a version of a report made by a teacher member of the management group of the Warwick University secondary PGCE mentoring scheme, and reflects the views of the schools' mentors[1] together with those of the University's professional and subject tutors at the end of the first year of the pilot. The views of each group of people consulted are placed together, because this is thought to be the most helpful and most accessible way into the scheme for those institutions interested in how the Warwick pilot scheme for school-based teacher education worked in 1992–93.

The Warwick pilot scheme is divided between subject and professional studies based at the University, and block teaching practices of six weeks in the Autumn Term and eight weeks in the Summer Term. Each of these blocks is preceded by a serial practice of several separate days to enable students, usually placed in schools in groups of eight, to be inducted into their schools. There is also further school experience in the Spring Term.

Responsibility for student teachers is shared between the University's professional and subject tutors and teachers acting as professional and subject mentors during teaching practices. In this chapter *tutor* signals someone from the University, and *mentor* signals someone from the schools. There has been joint training for mentors and tutors and some transfer of funding from University to schools to support the program.

At the heart of the scheme is the Record of Professional Achievement, referred to throughout this chapter as RoPA. It is a series of documents by means of which University tutors and school mentors record a student teacher's progress through a process of review and target-setting.

Summary of Opinions of Professional Tutors

The course as a whole, in its pilot year (1993), has had many successes. There is widespread agreement that this has been an outstandingly good cohort of student teachers — in subject and education group work, in assignments and in the classroom — and the nature of the scheme itself must have had some part to play in this pleasing performance. There have been favourable comparisons with the previous PGCE course, and the student teachers themselves have overwhelmingly been satisfied customers. The more structured and common format of education seminars has strengthened the scheme. It has been more satisfactory working with students placed as groups in schools who have been able to support and enrich each other and draw more coherent inferences from their shared experience. Larger groups are also more worthwhile for schools. Even though the scheme is a pilot project with all the teething problems that that entails, the vast majority of people involved have had a vision of what the scheme is striving to be.

There has been commitment to the spirit of RoPA but there are some problems with processes and documentation. These can be grouped under three headings: structure, timing and expertise. The format and structure should be simplified. The timing and content of the prescribed interviews may sometimes be inappropriate; for example, asking students to reflect on past sessions when they are more concerned with preparing for a forthcoming practice. Professional tutors have generally devoted enough time to RoPA. These tutors from the University evolved a very satisfactory system of interviewing student teachers in their schools, even if they were not able to see them teach. Even so, some students have been unconvinced by the process and have not prepared themselves sufficiently for their interviews with university tutors. If RoPA became more student-driven, student teachers might feel more ownership of it. There has been some uncertainty about the process and it has been used by different people in different ways. This is confusing for students, and has undermined confidence. All of the documentation may not have been completed but the process of review and target-setting was completed, and RoPA has led to more meaningful discussions. In the view of one university tutor, RoPA's main benefit was to make university tutors set aside time for proper structured conversations with each student.

As far as school-University partnership is concerned there is some misunderstanding in schools about tutor — particularly subject tutor — support. Professional tutors' visits to schools were to link up with professional mentors, to discuss their programs, rather than, as in the past, to see student teachers teach. Schools appear not fully to understand the implications of the present pilot scheme and the government's intentions for initial teacher training as outlined in DfE *Circular 9/92*, particularly the greatly increased responsibility which falls on schools and mentors.

In the pilot scheme, the involvement of teachers is better than in the past. It is more committed, purposeful and effective. The working parties set up after the February 5, 1993 training day, in which professional and subject tutors collaborated with their respective school counterparts, have done a great deal of work towards clarifying responsibilities, setting common standards and sharing good practice and knowledge of each other's programs of work. This has directly addressed the question often asked by mentors: 'What have the students been taught so far and where should we begin?' It is felt essential for the University's and the schools' programs to be published, and agreed criteria to be monitored. Further work will be needed to develop and monitor the collaboration.

The balance of time and responsibility between the University and partner schools is about right now. More time could be allocated for University tutors to see their students and to liaise with mentors. University-based time offers students a range of approaches which can then be taken up in individual schools. Student teachers also valued the Spring Term school experience, which gave them yet further insights into dimensions of schooling.

Lack of resources is always a difficulty. Having University tutors working extensively with and in individual schools is fine in principle, but uneconomic in the present circumstances of transfer of funding to schools. Compromises will have to be sought to enable the triangular relationship between student teachers, mentors and tutors to be developed. Consortia of schools could share expertise and moderate each other's work, and tutors and groups of student teachers could meet mid-practice. Whilst it might be difficult to fund any more in the way of *subject* tutor visits, it might make sense to give more *professional* tutor time to enable classroom visits to be made. In situations of difficulty it is a serious disadvantage for a professional tutor not to have seen a student teach. Remote diagnosis of teaching problems is risky.

There are some concerns about mentor roles. While mentoring departments can offer a range of teaching styles and approaches, the training of mentors needs a lot more consideration. It should be more substantial, structured and flexible. There was some agreement with the idea of accrediting mentors after training. Skills of empathy and sensitive negotiation are vital under the new scheme and student teachers have a right to expect them in all their mentors and tutors. At present there are shortcomings in some schools, for example, some teachers tend to protect students too much when it comes to assessment. Again, schools tend to appoint the Deputy Headteacher as the professional mentor and this could be a mistake. More time is needed to look after a group of eight student teachers than busy Deputy Headteachers have.

It is fortunate that there is a great diversity in the schools available to take part. Herein lies a dichotomy. The richness of diversity, which is a great strength of the Warwick University/school placement system, has to be seen in relation to a basic student teacher entitlement. Professional tutors are asking if individual schools have a wide enough range or is there a danger of parochialism. Tutors and student teachers may perceive unevenness between schools, and there is an implication for ongoing training, monitoring and selection. Another issue to take into account is the willingness of schools to participate. Schools must be part of the scheme because they wish to be, not because they have had their arms twisted when the University is desperate for placements.

Professional tutors are responsible for writing the University's references and, because they have not seen students teach, they are obliged to rely heavily on reports from the professional and subject mentors, who may themselves have been asked by the student for references. There is a danger that references making substantially the same points may be submitted on a student, which a prospective employer may find unsatisfactory, if not suspicious. Finally, there must be a proper mechanism for the University to take up shortcomings with schools; for schools to complain about problems with individual tutors or with the administration of the scheme; and for students to voice concerns about any aspects of the course.

Summary of Opinions of Professional Mentors

It is reassuring that everyone agrees with the principle of RoPA. What is needed, as the following comments indicate, is refinement of detail. Professional mentors in schools found that dealing with RoPA for up to eight student teachers was burdensome. The targets set in RoPA at the end of the first practice were useful, and second school mentors were able to focus the induction interview on them, and then review progress in a later interview. Everyone would like to see an improved version of RoPA — slimmed down, simplified and with clearer assessment guidelines. Some thought that there was a general problem of the University's issuing too much documentation. There was agreement that student teachers do not value RoPA as much as might be hoped, largely because it is too complex and has not been used systematically enough and with confidence by mentors and tutors. Students remained suspicious of and to a degree inhibited by the basic ambiguity of the concept of a record of achievement, and perhaps this is underlined by the document's very title. Is this a formative document for a student to record developmental stages, including problems and failures; or is it a summative one which stands as an assessment? If both, it is not crystal clear which part is which, and who the immediate and eventual audiences are. If parts of RoPA are being used for reference writing, has the student teacher's permission been sought?

There is a variety of practice when it comes to writing final reports on student teachers. Some mentors are producing traditional reports which are finalised after being shown briefly in draft form to student teachers for their comments. At the other end of the spectrum, some students are being asked to draft assessments on their own performance, which the mentor then uses in writing a report. If students are to be responsible for drafting their own reports, they will need support — and more than a token negotiation. Most students probably find commenting on their own performance quite difficult in the first teaching practice, but should be more confident in doing so in the second. Ideally both parties need to contribute fully. Meaningful negotiation would then become the key to the whole process of mentoring.

Student teachers move from their first school to a second school. Inter-school partnerships, necessary to make the move trouble-free, have been variable in quality, and dissemination of good practice in this area, as in others, will help make the second year of the pilot more productive. It is important that information from first to second practice schools should be of good quality and arrive promptly. It could be helpful for the University to act as a clearing house. Mentors from various schools have made contact with each other on training days, and have visited each other's schools, sometimes accompanied by student teachers. These visits have been both social and informative. It seems particularly important for second practice mentors to have some knowledge of first practice schools, so that student teacher reports can be understood in context, and serial practice can be planned in the light of what students have already done. Students also say that a visit late in the first practice from or, even better, to the second practice mentor, helps dispel apprehensions and offset possibly damaging speculation about the differences between the two schools.

The only real caveat is that a student teacher who had a difficult or unsuccessful first practice, for whatever reason, would be glad of the chance of a fresh start second time round, and the prospect of further involvement of a first practice mentor might be unwelcome. The suggestion that first practice mentors should have some input into the final assessment of students needs to be treated with caution, although at face value it is an attractive idea as these mentors would be in a good position to see the development of the student over the whole course.

There have been some very positive comments about school–University partnership. One mentor described it as impressive. There has been a lot of paperwork but it has been of good quality and mainly in good time. It has been satisfying and exciting for teachers to have had a hand in shaping things during the pilot scheme, and further developments of the relationship are eagerly awaited. Another view was that partnership still needs to be developed. Teachers and student teachers still expect more University tutor involvement. Links need to be fostered but so far there is some perception that there has been too little contact with tutors. Mentors, however, envisage a continuing partnership based on each party's recognition that the other has something essential to contribute. Only one had contemplated a future as a training school without University partnership.

Several people thought that the course should not be divided up into discrete areas of responsibility, but should reflect a genuine collaborative partnership in which schools and university tutors work together throughout the whole year. The subject, professional and RoPA groups who have worked together during the Spring and Summer Terms have made progress towards this target. During the second year of the pilot there should be more teacher involvement in the University-based part of the course and more tutor involvement in the teaching practices.

Most mentors enjoyed the training days in July 1992 and February and July 1993, and thought that it was important for teachers to be involved. Mentors had benefited, especially relatively inexperienced ones who are not Heads of Department. Even those who did not enjoy the training days and thought the money could have been better spent, especially when funding of school-based work is seen as a problem, conceded that consultation with teachers was important both practically and symbolically. Those who have been able to give time to the working parties have enjoyed their involvement, and many who have not been able to afford the time would have liked to make a contribution.

The question of whole school awareness and attitudes has training implications. Schools involved in mentoring will need to increase the awareness of all their staff, not just those colleagues or departments directly involved. A proportion of 1993–94 funding to schools is dedicated to in-school training. Mentors have various ideas about how to approach this. Some will devote part of a whole-school training day to mentoring. Other ideas include support for those colleagues who are using their mentoring work in further degrees. Some schools are certainly hoping to recruit University expertise to help directly or indirectly with staff development. While head teachers and governors have been consulted and have given support to the pilot scheme, little has been done yet to publicise it to parents. Perhaps schools with their first year's experience behind them will feel confident enough to share their commitment with parents, pointing out the advantages as well as the responsibilities of being involved in training teachers.

During serial and block practices, professional mentors believe they achieved the key tasks of putting across the school's ethos and systems to their student teachers, as well as allowing them to progress quickly from observation via participation to autonomous teaching. Many said they had learned lessons about how to work with groups of students and what to include in seminars. Some mentors had been able to continue the program of work through the block practice. Others had done most of the sessions during the serial practice, and departments had then taken over student teachers almost completely. The University needs to facilitate the sharing of good ideas and practice, and to encourage schools to continue general teaching programs for student teachers during the whole practice, including opportunities for students to see work in departments other than their own. This is a chance they will not easily find again once they are in teaching posts. Work on curriculum vitae and interviews had been appreciated, and had given staff who would not otherwise have been involved a chance to work with student teachers.

Those student teachers who had benefited most from their school experience had not only had full programs, but had been encouraged to throw themselves into the life of the school through pastoral attachments, parents' evenings, training days, department and staff meetings, work experience visits and other activities which they will of course be expected to take part in as soon as they take up teaching posts.

Teachers, in order to be effective mentors, need to be trained and developed. Passing on their own practice, however good it may be, is not sufficient to the task. Teachers as mentors need to be able to analyse why some things work in some circumstances and for some people but not for others, and it may be quite hard for experienced teachers to do this, as they rely more on that very experience and intuition. Lone teachers may not be able to analyse dispassionately their own philosophy or practice or recommend a range of teaching approaches. A mentoring department working as a team offers some solutions, but there are major implications for ongoing training, development and monitoring for schools to share their mentoring experiences and expertise.

It has proved very satisfactory for departments to work as mentoring teams, and indeed much of the day-to-day work gets left to them. While this is a good thing, the teachers involved, most of whom will not have had any mentor training, need opportunities to develop and share their skills. There may also be differences of approach between one department and another in the same school, and while this may be acceptable in most cases, departments need to share their practice, so that differences do not become serious inconsistencies.

Professional mentors recognise that subject mentors do a lot of work with student teachers, and that finding time to do a thorough job can represent a real problem for them. Compared to first practice schools, where many subject mentors seemed to be Heads of Department, second practice schools had more mentors who were not Heads of Department, seeing the role very much as a developmental one for the teacher. There are many positive benefits for departments and schools as a whole. The skills of mentoring are similar to those of appraisal, and it has been helpful to have the two initiatives coming together. Compared with the previous PGCE scheme, in which students in school were under the supervision of university tutors, the pilot scheme is a lot of work for teachers, but there are advantages in dealing with larger groups of student teachers, although more than one school found that eight students take up a lot of space in a small staffroom.

Assessment of student teachers by mentors was not perceived by most people to be problematic. Some said they would appreciate more guidance, especially with weaker students, but in cases of difficulty, help was available from university tutors.

The structure of the course as a whole is seen as very satisfactory. The balance of time between school and University is felt to be fine as it is, although some schools would welcome the chance to be involved in the parts of the course (at University) which are not devoted to teaching practice. There was also the suggestion that perhaps assignments could be more school-based. The school-based scheme is thought to be better than the one it replaces. Having a practice in two different schools was thought particularly useful. One mentor remarked on the difference between those of his student teachers who had come from one first practice school and those from another. One group had been rigorously trained (in lesson planning, for example), whilst another group had been less closely supervised. The former group settled into their second practice more quickly and with more assurance than the latter. This illustrates the advantages of early training, even though the student teachers may not have appreciated it at the time.

Many benefits to the school were seen. Students brought with them enthusiasm, hard work and commitment, new ideas, extra hands, a breath of fresh air into a school where newly qualified teachers have been rarely seen of late. They had become part of the school and had involved themselves in a whole range of activities and functions.

Summary of Opinions of Subject Tutors

The subject tutors were those most concerned with the RoPA process. For them, it did not go entirely as planned. Some tutors found RoPA disappointing in terms of what students brought to it and got out of it. If it were a more flexible document and if eventually Local Education Authority (LEA) or school Newly Qualified Teacher (NQT) co-ordinators are expecting to see a RoPA action plan, student teachers will be more motivated to complete it. Tutors believe the document needs to be more student-driven. They also believe it is important for all who use it to be surer of it. Student teachers do not have enough initial training on using ROPA and identifying and assessing competencies. They do not have enough experience to assess themselves. A RoPA interview in the Spring Term would be more useful when students could compare course with practice. In the Summer Term some tutors offered their students an interview at the university or at their school. What the student teachers wanted and in some cases got was a lesson observation with feedback and a discussion.

RoPA did create an atmosphere of confidence and honesty, and even though commitment to the documentation itself tailed off in the Summer Term, the structure had been valuable in involving student teachers in the assessment of their own progress. The quality of involvement varied, and not all tutors found the RoPA format easy to translate into discussions. The fact that it is presented in separate sections militates against the overall unity of the course. They look forward to the new document which promises to be clearer, simpler, better-constructed and more flexible.

To overcome the problem of ambiguity identified by student teachers (is it to be used for professional development or for assessment?), sections need to be colour-coded or otherwise very clearly marked so there is no doubt which sections are formative and which summative and public.

One tutor was not sure that RoPA is appropriate for post-graduates. Its purpose may need to be redefined, and it should include assignment work which illustrates the development of professional skills. It needs to be more of a portfolio than a set of opinions — something more challenging and illustrative of skills and achievements.

The school–University partnership is still developing. It worked better with second practice schools mainly because more time was available in the Summer Term for visits and because contacts had been made between mentors and tutors on the February 1993 training day. Tutors need enough time to remain familiar with the schools they are working with. While this does not need as much time as used to be spent under the terms of the previous scheme, it does need more visits than are officially allocated now. Tutors should still have involvement, otherwise they will lose touch with schools. With the change of the University tutor's role, student teachers felt abandoned during their teaching practices and requested more visits which would improve relationships with students and mentors. University tutors undoubtedly have an important part to play during teaching practices, but school visits are not cost-effective, so some compromises will have to be sought. More visits, and the whole future of the scheme, depend on financial implications.

Working groups and collaboration with teachers have been excellent, although teacher response was small. University tutors will be trying next year to foster more continuous collaborative work, rather than perpetuate a compartmentalised course. For instance, more use could be made of teacher input during the Spring Term subject sessions. Already the working parties have gone some way towards defining what teaching of students needs to be done by schools. The future of the scheme is in partnership, with each side acknowledging that their partner's contribution is vital.

University tutors reported that they found the training days useful in renewing contacts and making new ones, so that when they went out into schools they were not 'going in cold'. They found a high level of commitment by mentors. Most visits revealed some clearly set out programs, but in some schools encouragement was needed. Most student teachers were being well supported, and only one mentor made it clear that he was an unwilling draftee. An often-asked question was: 'We will be seeing you again, won't we?' followed by disappointment that no further visits were allocated. Many mentors did not fully understand their own new responsibilities. Students now should be taught by mentor teachers about general educational issues during practice. In many cases further visits were made by the University tutor in the Summer Term, not to see students teach but to discuss successes and failures of the pilot scheme.

Student teachers' experiences have been varied, with differences between schools and between departments within the same school. This is by no means surprising or even undesirable, but it is important that school and departmental contexts are taken into account in assessing students. The question is, how can the schools themselves judge this effectively? There would be positive benefits for schools in consortium arrangements, sharing expertise and resources. It is crucial to draw schools into training, monitoring and moderation.

The most important thing is that student teachers are satisfied with their experiences this year, and that the Warwick secondary PGCE scheme has much better support systems (potentially and actually) than those in many other institutions. There are many positive benefits. Because of the working parties' activities, there was a new atmosphere on the last training day in July 1993; and because of schools' greater responsibilities, student teachers have been more absorbed into their practice schools.

Tutors are aware that there have been a lot of meetings and papers as part of the training program. The single training days in February and July 1993 were thought to have been more useful than the pairs of days in July 1992 which were thought to be unfocused, although probably this was necessary in the consultative stage. There is a need now to build on what has been done, and to consolidate the competency-based documents produced by the working parties. Future training should concentrate on subject and education areas rather than on holding big 'jamborees'. University tutors need to support mentors and facilitate their work with student teachers in lesson planning, evaluation and use of teaching practice files. During the coming year work needs to be done collaboratively on supervision, planning, then subject application, worked out in clear steps.

Progression during the serial practice was very satisfactory, with most students able to become increasingly involved in teaching from an early stage. Only a few felt the need for a longer serial practice. Observation itself might be more focused, with the student observing a lesson which the teacher then discusses and evaluates. Some students were anxious that they were not given a teaching timetable until very late.

This year (1992–93) has been a learning experience for all concerned, not just for the student teachers. With the change in mentor and tutor roles, it is to be expected that both sides have some reservations. Tutors have identified some inconsistencies among mentors, not so much in quality as in commitment and time available for the tasks. Some mentors' work is too unfocused, and they are still expecting as much University tutor support as under the previous scheme, to such an extent that student teachers in a few schools have felt less than fully supported. There is not yet a genuine triangular relationship among student, mentor and tutor, and the mentor/tutor link is in some cases still weak. As a result, in the Summer Term, some tutors were bypassing mentors and working directly with student teachers. It would be helpful to have one accredited mentor in each partnership school who would help colleagues develop in a consistent way, and foster teamwork.

One particular problem for mentors is how to gauge a reasonable standard. The answer is to do with experience. Tutors used to learn their craft from another experienced supervisor, and had the opportunity to see a broad sample of lessons across the curriculum in both primary and secondary schools. This experience provided reference points for future supervision and assessment. Mentors working from scratch and with much more limited experience have found some difficulty. It is important to recognise that the skills of the classroom are not the same as those of a mentor. Mentors have a teaching job to do, not merely a supervisory one. They must be able to identify the important things in student teachers' performance, evaluate their needs in the form and content of lessons, and offer a range of strategies, not merely a successful alternative.

Some University tutors believe their role has been impoverished, and see that their situation could become even worse. Others, more positively, see a continuing but changed role for tutors in overview, support, training and organising. They believe that they can help more in the Autumn Term by working with students on preparation for observation and evaluation of lessons. They see the university-based part of the course as an economical use of time, and would greatly regret that time being reduced. Tutors need to maintain links with schools. It is important for the theory/practice divide not to be widened.

As far as the course as a whole is concerned, there have been benefits for University tutors which have been real but intangible. Working with groups has been more motivational, and some tutors have worked with more student teachers, which has had disadvantages as well as advantages.

Subject tutors observe that student teachers on the whole feel that they have gained a good deal from the course. They have been absorbed into their schools and have valued the support they have received from tutors and mentors. They have been glad to be part of a successful trial, and have enjoyed being part of a supportive group during practices. The basic model and structure of the PGCE course is a good one. The present time balance is correct, and having less University-based subject time would be problematical. The university time is needed to give balance, a wide range of ideas and the means of making comparisons. Student teachers need time to step back and reflect. Without the University-based time, they would lose some dimensions of their development. One beneficial adjustment might be a mid-practice recall to share experiences so far, check on achievements and targets, and offer reassurance and counselling where necessary.

It has been encouraging to see that most people believe in the underlying principles of the pilot scheme while acknowledging that the scheme has had some confusions and problems. Developments have not been disasters. The success of the scheme has depended on the willingness of mentors and tutors to make the scheme work, the sense of doing something new, the RoPA atmosphere and collaboration. The University and its partner schools have together accomplished a major step forward. Another is now needed.

Other areas of concern were identified. There are problems ahead in the University's retention of its role. In order to cater for student teachers' different competencies, supported self-study may be a way forward. Subject work needs tailoring to student teacher need — for example, information technology experience. There are major course development issues here. Schools did not have enough time or encouragement to work on teaching practice files and on things like lesson preparation. Contractual arrangements must be more specific and commitments agreed. Too many assumptions appear to be being made about graduates' subject knowledge. What they did in their degree courses and what they have to be able to do in school, even within their own discipline, are very different. Student teachers cannot teach with conviction if they are not sure of their own subject competence. These are issues for the university to address.

Summary of Opinions of Subject Mentors

The sense of partnership between school and University is real, much more so than it has ever been in the past, and there has been much satisfaction in the collaboration. Those mentors who have been able to join the working parties have valued the opportunity. Communications have been good, and some tutors have put in much more time than officially allocated. Visits from University tutors have been welcome, and mentors have been particularly glad for tutors to visit lessons when this has been possible. More tutor visits should be allocated. Students want them and without sufficient time being allocated to it, partnership

will not grow. University tutors need time to become and remain familiar with departmental styles in different schools, as well as to make at
least one lesson observation per student teacher.

The RoPA used in the first year of the pilot has been perceived by
subject mentors in schools as flawed and ambiguous, but the proposed
changes sound encouraging. The general feeling amongst subject
mentors was that RoPA was the right thing to be doing, and that as well
as revision and clarification, what was needed was a thorough briefing
and crystal clear set of instructions for all those using it. Many subject
mentors have found RoPA reasonably straightforward. They have been
concerned with reporting on lesson supervisions. Summaries of such
reports were drafted, then discussed with student teachers. Weaker
students sometimes had difficulty in reconciling themselves to what
was said, and careful negotiation was necessary. Some reports had
been traditional and need to be more consultative. Some schools are
promising themselves to work on this more next year.

There was contact between mentors from partner schools during
the February 1993 training day, which was appreciated. In many cases
this has been the only contact, distance between schools being a major
factor. For some mentors there have been other activities — for example,
working parties — and others are planned. The contrast between schools
is valuable; and satisfactory information was passed on, together with
useful action plans.

Mentors were often surprised by the lack of student teachers'
knowledge of basics — preparation, planning, marking, assessment,
and the National Curriculum. They expected more expertise than students showed in the second teaching practice.

Mentors are aware of positive benefits in the pilot scheme for all
concerned — student teachers, teachers and pupils. Some teachers have
seen benefits in the shape of help with schemes of work and information
technology development within subject work. Mentoring has contributed to professional development of staff and teambuilding in staffrooms.
Colleagues have been encouraged to work for further qualifications
and higher degrees. There are benefits to teachers in that they are
obliged to examine their own practice. Having a pair or a group of student teachers is supportive for them and makes seminars and other
work more worthwhile. Mentors believe there is a high level of commitment to mentoring within their schools, and that there is whole
school awareness and support, but would be glad of further awareness-
raising and development on a school training day.

The models used on the three training days in July 1992 and
February 1993 were right for many mentors who thought it necessary

to avoid the idea that there was a rigid and predetermined plan to work to. The evolutionary process and genuine consultation with teachers were appreciated and gave all concerned a sense of ownership, although a few mentors would have preferred a more direct approach.

The framework of serial and block practice appears to have worked well, with student teachers receiving a thorough introduction to the school context and rapid progression towards independent teaching. In some schools observation continued during the block practice, with students spending time in other departments. Many schools (and student teachers) feel that the second serial practice is too long. During the block practice some students have been involved in team teaching, either with each other or with other teachers. It is felt that students should have worked with classes who are engaged on examination or standard attainment test work, if necessary as a support or team teacher. After all they will in all probability be responsible for such classes in their first year of teaching.

The role of the mentor is a developmental one. It is a professional, reflective process. It helps prevent teachers from becoming complacent and stale because in working with student teachers they have to re-examine, defend and maybe change their own ideas and practice. Departments and faculties have mentored as a team with the subject mentor acting as coordinator and have been able to offer a range of styles and feedback. If the whole department contributes to the mentoring process they share the task. Mentoring is a lot of work and responsibility, especially for a small department. Co-operation also gives teachers other than the mentor contact with student teachers, helps build a team and enriches student teachers' experiences.

Teachers have taken their responsibilities seriously. They can see the links with teacher appraisal, and the style of feedback to students has changed. Consistent approaches to the mentoring task come from the meeting together of mentors and their school colleagues. Making the mentor role, tasks and timetable quite clear means that in situations of pressure the job can be done without timewasting uncertainty.

In the course as a whole, the balance of time and responsibility is thought to be about right as it is now. More University tutor involvement in the school-based element, and more teacher (and pupil) involvement in the University-based part of the course would correct the tendency to discrete divisions in the present structure.

Mentors think that the school-based scheme compares well with the previous system, concentrating as it does on teaching skills and practicalities. There will always be a place for the University to relate these to a theoretical base and give opportunities for reflection and comparison. The product at the end of the pilot scheme was better than in previous years, and there is general agreement that the student teachers this year were of a very high standard in all respects. Some were good to begin with and others made great progress.

Conclusion

Those mentors and University tutors interviewed have offered a range of good ideas and constructively critical observations, and some of the points identified have already been addressed by the working parties — issues such as resourcing, training, accreditation and monitoring remain as priorities. The evident commitment of all those involved in the basic principle of school-based teacher education balance the criticisms, which are mostly of a practical nature and easily remedied.

I hope that this honest appraisal of one institution's initial teacher training scheme in a transitional phase will be of use to others involved in mentoring and in the vast changes taking place in the training of pre-service teacher education students.

Note

1 The positions in the Warwick team are those of professional tutor and subject tutor, both of whom are university staff, and professional mentor and subject mentor both of whom are school staff. The 'professional' team members are the general education experts, and the 'subject' team members, are, as the name implies, subject specialists.

Chapter 9

An Overview

Terry Field

Teacher education is changing; it is evolving. The complexities of teaching have always presented a challenge as to how best beginning teachers can be guided, educated and trained in acquiring the skills necessary to provide quality educational experiences for the children in their classes. The current wave of change has focused on an analysis of teacher competencies as a means of seeking to address the needs of student teachers as individual learners and to enhance the quality of teaching generally. The move to school-based teacher education in England is competencies-driven, as is shown in the DfE circulars that list competencies for beginning teachers (see Chapter 1). The similar move in Australia has as one of its precursors, lists of teaching competencies for beginning teachers. There are some who resist the competency base of school-based teacher education, yet the assessment and progress documents of the four case studies in the book use them to their own ends. As long as the complexities of the teaching task are not lost in the imposed uniformity of a list of competencies, such lists can provide a useful focus on the elements of teaching.

Teacher educators have been experimenting with different course patterns for many years, all too often, however, without giving due concern to student teachers' views and feelings about their experiences. We believe that when making decisions about the *practicum* it is wise to listen to the voices of the student teachers themselves, as they are the ones who experience the stresses and traumas of growing into being a teacher. The students whose journals were reviewed in Chapter 2 express a need for more of a school base to their pre-service teacher education. That chapter clearly demonstrated the wide range of discourses used in the thinking of student teachers as they address the challenges of the classroom and the needs of young learners. The realities of classroom teaching appear to stimulate their thinking very positively in the development of strategies to improve their own responses in the classroom. This would point to the need for more time in school for student teachers.

The separation of school and university in the pre-service education of teachers has led to misunderstandings and ignorance of the role that each played. This is outlined in Chapter 3. Teachers in schools took on themselves a socialising role assuming that the theoretical areas of the course were to be dealt with only in the university. However, in the past, time in the classroom for student teachers was short. In the three or four weeks that students had in schools, they were able only to spend some time with classes briefly 'trying their hand' at a few lessons. Rarely was there time for reflection on practice or reflection on the relationship of that practice to the theory learned at university. Rarely did their short *practicum* allow them to develop a close rapport with their pupils as they had been told was necessary. Few teachers or university staff involved in teacher education in the last twenty years would deny that practice teaching sessions have been fragmented in preparing neophyte teachers to meet the constantly changing demands of schools. The essential message of this book is that there are signs of a better approach developing. This involves having student teachers immersed in school for much longer periods than previously, and giving to their mentor teachers a greater responsibility in their training and education.

The roles and responsibilities of mentors were discussed in Chapter 4. Mentor teachers are pivotal to a school-based program of teacher education. It is they who can most clearly help beginning teachers explore the nuances of the theory-practice interface. The immediacy of their guidance is critical, and who better than they to construct a curriculum for the *practicum*. As exemplified in Chapters 5–8, the real partnerships that are being developed between schools and universities are bringing a new look to pre-school teacher education. Teachers no longer have a subsidiary role, but are key teacher educators, with university tutors, in providing essential student teacher support.

Teacher education, then, will become more context sensitive. It is becoming embedded in individual school contexts. The learning experiences of teacher education students in schools could be different from each other. Schools and classrooms are unique, and school-based teacher education can capitalise on this uniqueness. All classroom teachers have particular strengths, and so develop and shape a learning environment for their pupils which reflects their own characteristics and philosophies. Clearly, then, sequences of experiences in the *practicum* conceived by different teachers will reflect differences among them. Experiences of student teachers will vary greatly. With student teachers being immersed for some 60 per cent of their time in different contexts, students from the same HEI could be shaped by markedly different experiences if the partnership between school and university is not strong. There are potential benefits and dangers in this diversity. Both need to be monitored by the partnership between the university and the schools.

It is clear that the English experience has already demonstrated that the development of true partnerships between schools and HEIs has resulted in a much more open approach to teacher education. University teacher educators now must dialogue with mentor teachers about the school experience programs for student teachers, and reach agreement as to how responsibilities for those programs will be shared. This has called for a much more precise articulation of programs between schools and HEIs than has ever been achieved in the past. For teachers, these expanded responsibilities have brought a new sense of direction and purpose in the training of teachers. It has also brought the worry of added work and the need for further resourcing of schools to cope with the added task. For teacher educators in higher education it has meant a change of focus onto guiding mentoring teachers in their development of the mentoring skills called for in the new arrangements. Meetings between university and staff and teachers are necessary to organise and plan effective programs. This new shared experience has created a more participatory and collaborative environment for teacher education. Both sides benefit from the expertise of the other.

When universities controlled the major part of teacher education programs, no matter how hard they tried, lecturers could never achieve the realism of the experience provided during a *practicum*. Student teachers have always seen the classroom as the most powerful learning environment. However, their periods of *practicum* were so short that they would find that their contact with pupils was coming to an end just as they were beginning to win their confidence and trust, and to feel that they were beginning to teach effectively. The greater exposure of student teachers to the real world of the classroom has the potential to create a new breed of reflective teachers, especially as the collaborative target-setting flows through from the *practicum* to the induction year of teaching.

The benefits of school-based programs of teacher education go even further than those outlined above. There are real benefits for schools and teachers. Wideen and Hopkins (1984) asked teachers questions about the extent to which they learn new skills and gain new ideas from students and are able then to implement them in the classroom. The questions are pertinent today. Do teachers perceive any growth or change in themselves? Do they become more self-critical? Do they feel less isolated with their problems? Do instructional changes and organisational changes in the classroom occur as a result of the student teacher's presence? Can they specify anything that they do now that they did not do before they had a student teacher to supervise? Do they find their work more challenging now? The answers to these questions were unequivocally positive. Teachers answering similar questions in the study recorded in Chapter 3 gave their own professional development as one of the reasons for accepting students to supervise.

Mentoring also opens up a new career pathway for teachers. David Reid's chapter (Chapter 5) records how this is occurring in one setting. Senior teachers can take over the role of co-ordinator of practice teaching in the school, or liaison officer between school and university. Already roles such as those of Chris Kellett and Martin Robinson are in place. Teachers value the chance to have 'mentor' on their *curriculum vitae*.

Supervision was a relatively powerless role for a teacher to accept compared with the role of teachers as mentors. The change is a dramatic one. Teachers as mentors are truly empowered as they share the responsibility for programming the curriculum for the *practicum*. The English experience is already clearly identifying such outcomes. The enhancement of career pathways for teachers can include the accreditation of this involvement as mentors as part of a higher degree program. And at the school level, the skills developed by mentor teachers should enable them better to join in peer appraisal and assessment — a process that is becoming increasingly important in schools.

So, mentoring students brings benefits for the teachers and the schools involved. It is interesting that Zeichner (1990) has identified teachers who undertake mentoring as usually those who are happy to enquire into their own teaching practice. They are reflective teachers who are well-equipped to engender reflective habits in their student teachers if they are given sufficient time to be an effective influence on them. Mentors, according to Zeichner, see themselves as scholars, innovators, researchers and, as suggested above, as reflective practitioners. They feel that they have something to pass on to students. The practitioners' observations in Chapters 5–8 provide sound testimony of the benefits that schools can gain from an increased emphasis on school-based teacher education.

More Recently . . .

Since the plan for this book was conceived and after the contents of it were drafted, proposals for further changes for an increased emphasis on school-based teacher education have been announced for England and Wales.

In June 1993, a draft circular (DfE, 1993a) concerning the initial training — pre-service education — of primary teachers appeared from the office of the Secretary of State for Education. This document states the following proposals:

- tough new criteria which all training courses must meet, focusing on the subject knowledge and teaching skills new teachers require to be effective in the classroom;
- a greater role for schools, which are best placed to help student teachers develop and apply practical teaching skills;
- a continuing need for study in higher education institutions of the subject knowledge necessary for sound teaching of the National Curriculum;
- a greater diversity of courses, including in particular:
  - a new three-year, six subject BEd to prepare teachers for work across the primary curriculum;
  - a new one-year course for those with experience of working with children, preparing them to teach nursery and infant pupils;
  - courses preparing teachers to work as subject specialists

The language is clear. Difficult though school-based primary teacher education appeared to be to teachers and teacher educators in prospect, especially in comparison with the education of secondary teachers, these reforms will continue. The proposed compliance date in England and Wales is 1 September 1996. The justification offered is an improvement in the quality and relevance of ITE as a whole, and a raising of the standards in schools together with achieving greater 'cost effectiveness'. The penalty for non-compliance is a denial of Qualified Teacher Status (QTS) for student teachers successfully completing programs which do not meet the criteria. Many also see threats in this document of a continuing de-professionalising of teaching as instanced in the proposed one-year course cited above in the 'greater diversity' of provisions.

For teachers and teacher educators in Australia some of the trends observable in the United Kingdom are already recognisable as 'kites' that have been flown to varying extents by their state departments in recent years. Combined with this, the continuing and inexorable pressure from the Commonwealth Government and other parties to 'unstitch' the present (national) Practice Teaching Supervision Award signals possible similar extensive changes to teacher education — both secondary and primary — in Australia in future years.

Even more recently in the United Kingdom, the Green Paper, published early in September 1993, has detailed changed funding arrangements to reinforce the policy to achieve a greater involvement of schools in the initial education of teachers. The suggestions here include the possible offering of teacher education programs by schools in their own right, apparently without any involvement of HEIs. Further, the Teacher Training Agency proposed in the Green Paper is likely to be charged with responsibility for distributing education research funds in England. The separation that this would create of education research and teacher education from mainstream higher education funding arrangements can be seen as another declaration of the intent of the (UK) Government to force through their agenda of change.

As indicated above in discussion of the draft circular, new patterns of ITE are being considered in the United Kingdom. When speaking in June 1993, the Secretary of State for Education is reported as suggesting that in some schools and for some courses higher education involvement is not necessary; a proposal that the Green Paper reinforces. While there are some reservations here the statement clearly indicates that the present pathways for the professional preparation of teachers are under threat.

It is a matter of judgment as to whether this agenda for change will achieve the desired and stated goals — as with much educational change, only time will tell. The heartening aspect of all of this is that the transformation of secondary teacher education in the UK has actually stimulated new ways of thinking about preparing young people for the challenges of classroom teaching. The information provided by David Read, Chris Kellett, Chris Husbands and Martin Robinson in Chapters 5 to 8 is clearly on the side of new paradigms, exciting potential and enhanced quality — in the education both of student teachers and of their pupils.

This book has documented some of these changes with the aim of helping teachers and others to understand the benefits that can flow from a greater involvement of schools in the initial education of teachers. Change is always challenging but, clearly, the case material cited here, in Chapters 5 to 8 in particular, indicates that the present moves to school-based initial teacher education, involving strong partnerships between secondary schools and HEIs, are not a backward step. They are certainly not a *re*-introduction of earlier strategies but rather new approaches to develop teachers who can address the challenges of working in today's, and tomorrow's, classrooms.

Challenging times call for creative solutions and seeking to revitalise teacher education through a greater involvement of schools in the process so that its graduates are able to enhance the quality of teaching is one such solution. The challenge for teachers in this strategy is to become, as well, a teacher educator or mentor, albeit in co-operation with staff from HEIs. For the latter, the challenge is different. Their work must develop not only strong partnerships with their co-operating primary and secondary schools, but also must be more specifically in research and in teacher education for further and technical education — and, even more importantly, for higher education itself.

References

ALEXANDER, R. (1984) 'Innovation and continuity in the initial teacher education curriculum', in ALEXANDER, R.J., CRAFT, M., and LYNCH, (Eds) *Change in Teacher Education: Context and Provision since Robbins*, London: Holt Rinehart and Winston.

BEARDON, T., BOOTH, M., REISS, M., and HARGREAVES, D. (1992) *School-led Training: The Way Forward*, Cambridge: Cambridge Education Paper, Cambridge University Department of Education.

BELL, A. (1981) 'Structure, knowledge and social relationships in teacher education', *British Journal of Sociology of Education*, **2** (1), pp. 3–25.

BOOTH, M.B. (1993) 'The effectiveness and role of the mentor in school: the students' view', *Cambridge Journal of Education*, **23** (2), pp. 185–99.

BRITZMAN, D.P. (1991) *Practice Makes Practice: A Critical Study of Learning to Teach*, New York: SUNY.

BROWN, G. (1985) 'The role of schools and teachers in teacher education' in FRANCIS, H. (Ed.) *Learning to Teach: Psychology in Teacher Education*, London: Falmer Press, pp. 56–65.

BROWN, M. and REID, D.J. (1990) 'Black for the people, green for the land, red for the blood of the martyrs: A case study of INSET in Malawi', *Research in Education*, **44**, pp. 94–107.

BROWN, S. and McINTYRE, D. (1986) 'How do teachers think about their craft?', in BEN-PERETZ, M., BROMME, R. and HALKES, R. (Eds) *Advances of Research on Teacher Training, Lisse, ISATT and Swets and Zeitlinger BV.*

CALDERHEAD, J. and GATES, P. (1993) *Conceptualizing Reflection in Teacher Development*, London: Falmer Press.

CARRUTHERS, J. (1993) 'The principles and practice of mentoring' in *The Return of the Mentor: Strategies for Workplace Learning*, London: Falmer Press, pp. 9–24.

CATE (1992) *School-Based Teacher Training: Notes of Guidance for Secondary Schools and Higher Education Institutions*, London: CATE.

CLARKE, K. (1992) Speech at the North of England Education Conference, January, London: Department for Education.

DARESH, J. and PLAYKO, M. (1993) 'Mentoring programmes as part of induction for beginning school principles, headteachers, and the education leaders', Paper presented at the International Conference 'Teacher Education: from Practice to Theory', July, Tel Aviv, Israel.

DEPARTMENT FOR EDUCATION (DfE) (1992) *Initial Teacher Training (Secondary Phase): Circular 9/92*, June, London: DFE.

DEPARTMENT FOR EDUCATION (DfE) (1993a) *The Initial Training of Primary School Teachers: New Criteria for Course Approval: Draft Circular*, June, London: DfE.

DEPARTMENT FOR EDUCATION (DfE) (1993b) *The Parent's Charter: Publication of Information about Secondary School Performance in 1993: Circular 4/93*, London: DfE.

DEPARTMENT OF EDUCATION AND SCIENCE (DES) (1992) *Reform of Teacher Education*, March, London: HMSO.

DEPARTMENT OF EMPLOYMENT, EDUCATION AND TRAINING (DEET) (1993) *Teaching Counts: A Ministerial Statement*, January, AGPS.

DLIN, E. and LEVI, R. (1993) 'Towards a collaborative model of staff development', Paper given at the International Conference, 'Teacher Education: From Practice to Theory', July, Tel Aviv, Israel.

DOBBINS, R. and WASLEY, D. 'Teachers as teacher educators: The impact of nomenclature on roles and relationships in the practicum', May, Magill: University of South Australia, (unpublished paper).

DUFFY, P. (1987) 'Student perceptions of tutor expectations for school-based teaching practice', *European Journal of Teacher Education*, **10** (3), pp. 261–8.

EDWARDS, A. (1992) 'Organisational issues for primary schools and teacher education: a shared vision', UCET Annual Conference November, Oxford.

ELLIOTT, J. (1985) 'Facilitating action research in schools: some dilemmas', in BURGESS, R.G. (Ed.) *Field Methods in the Study of Education*, London: Falmer Press.

ELLIOTT, J. (1990) *Action Research for Educational Change*, Milton Keynes: Open University Press.

ELLIOTT, J. (1991) 'Three perspectives on coherence and continuity in teacher education', unpublished paper, Universities Council for the Education of Teachers' conference.

ELLIOTT, J. (1993) *Reconstructing Teacher Education: Teacher Development*, London: Falmer Press.

EMANS, R. (1983) 'Implementing the knowledge base: redesigning the function of co-operating teachers and college supervisors', *Journal of Teacher Education*, **34** (3), pp. 14–17.

FEIMAN-NEMSER, S. and PARKER, M.B. (1992) 'Mentoring in context: a comparison of two US programs for beginning teachers', *National Centre for Research on Teacher Learning: Special Report*, Spring pp. 1–20.

FIELD, BARBARA (1992) *Post-Practicum Survey*, University of New England-Armidale (unpublished).

FISHMAN, A.R. and ROWER, E. (1989) 'Maybe I'm just not teacher material' *English Education*, **21** (2), pp. 92–109.

FROST, D. (1993) 'Reflective mentoring and the new partnership', in WILKIN, M. (Ed.) *Mentoring in Schools*, London: Kogan Page pp. 130–45.

FURLONG, V.J., HIRST, P.H., MILES, S. and POCKLINGTON, K. (1988) *Initial Teacher Training and the Role of the School*, Milton Keynes: Open University Press.

GARDNER, P. (1993) 'The early history of school based teacher training', in McINTYRE, D., HAGGER, H. and WILKIN, M. (Eds) *Mentoring: Perspectives on School-Based Teacher Education*, London: Kogan Page, pp. 21–36.

GILROY, D.P. (1992) 'The political rape of initial teacher education in England and Wales: a JET rebuttal', *Journal of Education for Teaching*, **18** (1), pp. 5–22.

HALLIWELL, S. (1988) 'The role of the PGCE method tutor', *Cambridge Journal of Education*, **15** (1), pp. 8–16.

HARGREAVES, D. and HAPHINS, D. (1991) *The Empowered School: The Management and Practice of Development*, London: Cassell.

HARGREAVES., D. (1992) *The Future of Teacher Education*, Hockerill Lecture, Hockerill Educational Foundation, Essex.

HMI (1991) *School-Based Initial Teacher Training in England and Wales: A Report by HM Inspectorate*, London: HMSO.

HIRST, P.H. (1983) 'Educational theory' in HIRST, P.H. (Ed.) *Educational Theory and Its Foundation Disciplines*, London: Routledge and Kegan Paul.

HUGHES, P. (Ed.) (1991) *Teachers Professional Development*, Hawthorn, Victoria: ACER.

HUSBANDS, C. (1993) 'Profiling student teachers: profiling and the beginnings of professional learning', in BRIDGES, D. and KERRY, T. (Eds) *Developing Teachers Professionally*, London: Routledge.

JUDGE, H. (1980) 'Teaching and professionalization: an essay in ambiguity' in HOYLE, E. and MEGARRY, J. (Eds) *World Yearbook of Education 1980: Professional Development of Teachers*, London: Kogan Page.

KAGAN, D.M. and ALBERTSON, L.M. (1987) 'Student teaching; perceptions of supervisory meetings' in *Journal of Education for Teaching*, **13** (1), pp. 49–59.

KEMMIS, K., COLE, P. and SUGGETT, D. (1983) *Orientations to Curriculum: Towards the Socially Critical School*, Melbourne: Victorian Institute for Secondary Education.

LAPOINTE, A.E., MEAD, N.A. and PHILLIPS, G.W. (1989) *A World of Differences: an International Assessment of Mathematics and Science*, Princeton, New Jersey: Educational Testing Service.

LAWLOR, S. (1990) *Teachers Mistaught: Education in Subjects or Training in Theories?*, London: Centre for Policy Studies.

LAWLOR, S. (1993) 'Who will teach the teachers: classrooms are the place to learn', *The Observer*, 14 March.

MACDONALD, B. (1984) 'Teacher education and curriculum reform: some English errors', Mimeo, CARE, University of East Anglia Address to Spanish Teacher Trainers, Malaga.

McINTYRE, D. (1980) 'The contribution of research to quality in teacher education', in HOYLE, E. and MEGARRY, J. (Eds) *World Yearbook of Education 1980: Professional Development of Teachers*, London: Kogan Page.

McINTYRE, D. (1987) 'Designing a teacher education curriculum from research and theory on teacher knowledge', in CALDERHEAD, J. (Ed.) *Teachers' Professional Learning*, Lewes: Falmer Press, pp. 97–114.

McINTYRE, D. (1990) 'The Oxford internship in terms of the Cambridge analytical framework', in FURLONG, V.J., WILKIN, M. and BOOTH, M.B. (Eds) *Partnership in Initial teacher education*, London: Cassell.

McINTYRE, D. and HAGGER, H. (1993) 'Teachers' expertise and models of mentoring' in McINTYRE, D. HAGGER, H. and WILKIN, M. (Eds) *Mentoring: Perspectives on School-Based Teacher Education*, London: Kogan Page, pp. 86–102.

McINTYRE, D., HAGGER, H. and WILKIN, M. (Eds) (1993) *Mentoring: Perspectives on School-Based Teacher Education*, London: Kogan Page.

McSHARRY, F.G. and REID, D.J. (1993) 'Quality assurance in multi-based secondary ITE: a position, a problem, a proposal', Paper given at the International Conference, 'Teacher Education: From Practice to Theory', July, Tel Aviv, Israel.

MUNRO, R. (1989) 'A case study of school-based innovation in secondary teacher education', unpublished PhD thesis, University of Auckland, New Zealand.

NATIONAL OFFICE OF OVERSEAS SKILLS RECOGNITION (1990) *The Identification and Assessment of Competencies: The Nursing Project and its*

Implications, Research Paper No. 4, Canberra: Australian Government Printer.

NATIONAL PROJECT ON QUALITY OF TEACHING AND LEARNING (1993) *The Development of National Competency Standards for Teaching*, Canberra.

NEW SOUTH WALES DEPARTMENT OF SCHOOL EDUCATION (1992) *Teacher Entry Level Competencies*, Version 5, May 8, Sydney.

NEW SOUTH WALES MINISTERIAL ADVISORY COUNCIL ON TEACHER EDUCATION AND QUALITY OF TEACHING (1993) *Areas of Competence for Beginning Teachers*, Sydney.

O'HEARE, A. (1988) *Who Teaches the Teachers?*, London: Social Affairs Unit.

O'HEARE, A. (1993) Article in the *Daily Mail*, June 7.

PARTINGTON, JOHN (1982) 'Teachers in school as practice supervisors', in *Journal of Education for Teaching*, **8** (3), pp. 262–73.

PENDRY, A. (1990) 'The Oxford internship and educational change', in BENSON, P. (Ed.) *The Oxford Internship Scheme: Integration and Partnership in Initial Teacher Education*, London: Calouste Gulbenkian Foundation.

REID, D.J., RYLES, A.P. and McSHARRY, F.G. (1994) London: HMSO
(a) The Science Curriculum
(b) Organisation and Resources in the Science Classroom
(c) Development and Learning in Science
(d) Assessment in Science
(e) Communication in the Science Lesson
(f) Science Practical work
(g) Valuing the Individual in Science
(h) Science Education and the Whole Curriculum

REID, D.J. (1993) 'Training for mentor empowerment: content and challenges', *Mentoring*, **1** (1), pp. 42–50.

REISS, M. and BEARDON, T. (1992) 'Exit criteria for initial teacher education' *Occasional Paper, 8 — Information Technology in Initial Teacher Training*, Warwick: NCET, pp. 65–77.

SCHON, D. (1983) *The Reflective Practitioner*, New York: Basic Books.

SCHUTZ, A. (1971) 'The stranger: an essay in social psychology', in COSIN, B.R., DALE, I.R., ESLAND, G.M., MACKINNON, D. and SWIFT, D.F. (Eds) *School and Society*, London: Routledge and Kegan Paul.

SMITH, R. and ALRED, G. (1993) 'The Impersonation of Wisdom in McINTYRE, D., HAGGER, H. and WILKIN, M. *Mentoring: Perspectives on School-Based Teacher Education*, London: Kogan Page.

STAKE, R. and EASLEY, J. (1978) *Case Structures in Science Education*, Washington DC: US Government Printing Office.

STENHOUSE, L. (1975) *An Introduction to Curriculum Research and Development*, London: Heinemann.

THIESSEN, D. (1992) 'Classroom-based teacher development', in HARGREAVES, A. and FULLAN, M.G. *Understanding Teacher Development*, London: Falmer Press.

TURNEY, C. (1993) Untitled, unpublished paper delivered at the National Practicum Conference, Macquarie University, Sydney.

University of Cambridge Department of Education (1992–1993) *Teaching Competences* (unpublished).

VAUGHAN, G. (1992) 'Profiling: a mechanism for professional development of students', *Cambridge Journal of Education*, **22** (2), pp. 163–75.

WALKER, J.C. (1992) *A General Rationale and Conceptual Approach to the Application of Competence Based Standards to Teaching*, a paper prepared for the national project on the quality of teaching and learning, May Canberra: University of Canberra Centre for Research in Professional Education.

WEBSTER, V. (1993) 'Supervising — what, how and why? The role and work of the supervising teacher', a paper presented at the *5th National Practicum Conference*, February, Maquarie University (unpublished).

WHITTY, G. and WILLMOTT, E. (1991) 'Competency-based teacher education: issues and concerns' *Cambridge Journal of Education*, **21** (3).

WIDEEN, M.F. and HOPKINS, D. (1984) 'Supervising student teachers: A means of professional renewal?' *The Alberta Journal of Educational Research*, **39** (1), pp. 26–37.

WILKIN, M. (1992) 'On the cusp: from supervision to mentoring in initial teacher training' in *Cambridge Journal of Education*, **22** (1), pp. 79–90.

WILKIN, M. (1993) 'The challenge of diversity', *Cambridge Journal of Education*, **23** (2), pp. 293–307.

WILLIAMS, G. and LODER, C. (1990) 'The importance of quality and quality assurance', in LODER, C. (Ed.) *Quality Assurance and Accountability in Higher Education*, The Bedford Way Series, London: Institute of Education.

WOODS, P. (1990) *Teacher Skills and Strategies*, London: Falmer Press.

ZEICHNER, K. (1990) 'Changing directions in the practicum: looking ahead to the 1990s', *Journal of Education for Teaching*, **16**, pp. 105–27.

ZEICHNER, K.M. and GORE, J.M. (1990) 'Teacher socialisation' in HOUSTON, W., HABERMAN, R.M. and SIKULA, J. (Eds) *Handbook of Research on Teacher Education: A Project of the Association of Teacher Educators*, New York: Macmillan Publishing Company, pp. 329–48.

Contributors

Barbara Field
Barbara Field is a Senior Lecturer and Co-ordinator of School Experience at the University of New England. She taught secondary English and ancient history in State and Independent Schools in New South Wales for 25 years before moving into teacher education. Her work as Co-ordinator of School Experience makes possible her research in her current interest in the *practicum* for student teachers.

Terry Field
Terry Field is Deputy Vice-Chancellor of the University of New England. He taught secondary science in state schools in New South Wales before moving into teacher education. This has been his chief professional interest during his career. He was Principal of the Armidale College of Advanced Education before its amalgamation in 1989 with the University of New England.

Chris Husbands
Chris Husbands is Lecturer in Education at the University of East Anglia, Norwich, England, having previously taught History in urban comprehensive schools in London, Norwich and Hertfordshire. He has teaching and research interests in History education, Information Technology and school-based teacher education. He has co-ordinated, with over 40 secondary schools, the development of the University's school-based secondary teacher education program between 1991 and 1993. He has written a number of papers on school-based teacher education, on student teachers' professional learning and on History education.

Chris Kellett
Christine Kellett is a specialist teacher of Personal and Social Education and Religious Education at Fulford School, York. After fourteen years as Head of Year, she has now become Coordinator of Initial Teacher Education at the school. A trained counsellor, Christine has taught the Careers Guidance and Counselling option course at the Department of

Educational Studies at the University of York for five years. She is now seconded part-time from school to the University where she acts as tutor on the Whole School Issue course of the Post-Graduate Certificate in Education.

David Reid

David Reid is currently Professor of Education and Director of Teacher Education at The University of Manchester, UK. David taught the biological sciences in secondary schools for twelve years, during which time he obtained a master's degree in curriculum studies. He joined The University of Manchester in 1977 and developed an interest in the psychology of children's learning in science, the subject of his doctorate. He has written widely in the fields of communication in classrooms, science education, special educational needs, and latterly in teacher education. He has held visiting professorships in a number of Universities and is interested in the way in which distance education packages can be used to support the delivery of school-based initial and INSET teacher training programs. His current research interests lie in comparative distance education in some African countries, America and the United Kingdom. He is a governor of several schools in the Manchester area and an experienced magistrate serving in both youth and adult criminal courts. He likes to keep in touch with colleagues by 'email' and invites you to share with him your ideas about mentoring in the Australian context. Please write to him at DREID2FS1.ED.MAN.AC.UK and he will reply.

Martin Robinson

Martin Robinson is a Deputy Headteacher at Ashlawn School, a large secondary school in Rugby, where he is mainly responsible for in-service training, staff development and appraisal. For the last two years he has also been working in the Department of Education at the University of Warwick as a tutor and as teacher member of a group set up to manage the introduction of an enhanced school-based Post-Graduate Certificate of Education, which completed its first pilot year in July 1993. His particular task was to act as Field Officer, visiting each of the University's partner secondary schools. These contacts resulted in two reports, the second of which is reproduced here in shortened form.

From September 1993 Martin is acting as Director (Forward Planning) Secondary PGCE at Warwick, with the task of putting a fully-fledged *Circular 9/92* PGCE in place for September 1994 and co-ordinating the production of substantial training and support materials for teacher mentors.

Index